STRATEGEEZ PUBLI.

I0036385

FINANCIAL
FREEDOM
ON YOUR CURRENT INCOME

How to put your finances
on autopilot in 5 easy steps ….
2.0 revised and updated

Michelle Smith

Totally revolutionize your finances in 90 days or less and stop
living payday to payday; live stress free and debt free.

FINANCIAL FREEDOM ON YOUR CURRENT INCOME

A practical guide to managing your money on "autopilot", set and forget. The Bill Banisher system takes the hassle out of budgeting and sets you up to prosper not just get by.

It eliminates the need for expense tracking and the problems of overspending.

DISCOVER

- ✓ Why 99.9% of budgets don't work and how to fix it in 5 easy steps.

HOW TO

- ✓ Eliminate overspending and lack of self-discipline once and for all.
- ✓ Fix relationship problems that manifest in your finances.
- ✓ Get out and stay out of debt the autopilot way.
- ✓ Build a solid financial foundation to begin investing in passive income investments

If you have "more month left at the end of your money" then once you get your foundations solid. We can explore simple easy ways to make more money, more choices and more freedom.

With my Bill Banisher system, because the cash flow is married to your budget there is no way you can overspend, there is also no need for self-discipline, which frees you up to think about the important things in life. Family and Fun.

Totally revolutionize your finances in 90 days or less

ABOUT THE AUTHOR

Michelle Smith

Being a little rebellious, wanting to do things her way, against the advice of her teachers and parents, Michelle left school at 15, began working and moved out of her family home. The school of hard knocks is where she learned her most valuable lessons.

Always looking for opportunity, Michelle began her first business at the age of 19. She wanted to be her own boss and was determined to be in control her own future. Fast forward to 2016, she has only worked for a boss for 12 months in 22 years.

However, life has not all been a bed of roses, and there have been a few major struggles along the way.

The biggest of these was when her husband Glen was unemployed for the first time in his life at 39. At the same time, Michelle was recovering from a three-and-a-half-year battle with chronic pain, which resulted in her losing her business.

With a massive 84% drop in income, a $300,000 mortgage and three young children to feed Michelle and Glen were backed against a wall. It was a matter of do something radical, or lose the lot.

By applying their systems building skills and using the banking system to their advantage they developed revolutionary new way of money management called Bill Banisher.

Once Bill Banisher was in place, there was never a day when going to the letterbox was a nasty surprise. While all around them people in the IT industry lost marriages and material possessions, they were free from the stress of bills and debt.

Friends of friends heard about Michelle's story and started asking her for help with their finances. Several couples were on the brink of bankruptcy, and in some cases, ready for divorce, but the Bill Banisher system totally neutralized the arguments about money! After a very short time, there was tangible evidence that they could really change their lives.

Karen, for example, was excited that after 13 years of marriage and no savings, she now had hope to one day buy a home. That was something not possible before.

Michelle shares with you how to get out of debt and set yourself up to prosper by showing you how to get your foundations solid and discover what inspires you in making YOUR money work for YOU. With her knowledge of money management, investing, strategy, business, sales and marketing Michelle will inspire you to get out of your comfort zone and change your financial future.

Lack of financial literacy affects every area of your life; if your children see you struggle with money, they will grow up with money problems also.

With this in mind, she has developed a simple, proven method to set your finances up so you will never have to worry or even think about them again.

Michelle is passionate about seeing change in the lives of people who are sick and tired of being controlled by their bills

and can't seem to get ahead.

TESTIMONIALS

Readers are finding Financial Freedom on Your Current Income an informative, quick and easy guide to getting their finances under control and working towards a brighter future.

Helen

Our finances were a mess – more money going out than coming in, massive debt and lots of stress. Both my husband and I work freelance, so we were never sure how much was going to be in the account, and because of this I avoided any structure or system as I could not conceive of how it would work with this irregular income.

I have to admit it has been one of the most confronting things I've done for a while!! Facing the reality of our situation was not easy, and some hard decisions had to be made.

The process took much less time than I anticipated, however fear and procrastination did prolong the agony!!

I now know exactly how much money I need per week to cover all expenses. I have a system in place that makes freelance income manageable, I don't feel guilty when I book the babysitter and go out because I know that I have enough in the allocated account to do it, and, having made the commitment to cut up our credit cards, we are now on the road to being debt free.

The best thing about it for me has been that now everything is "set", I don't have to micro manage the finances – it all takes care of itself!! I don't have to spend my time worrying about and juggling money, the stress in my marriage is over because we no longer need to blame each other for the mess, and I know we can start to move forward financially, which is exciting!!

Helen O'Connor

Actress.

STAR AND MARK

My husband and I have been implementing Michelle's budget system for three years now and have found it very easy to maintain.

Prior to this, we lived pay-check to pay-check and were always fearful to receive mail, just in case it was bills. It affected our marriage, and no matter what we tried in order to move ahead, we just could not get it together because unforeseen bills would eat each pay-check.

After working with Michelle, to our surprise, we had a monthly cash flow of $600.00 available to invest. We have never looked back; in fact, our monthly cash flow is now much more, and we are now doing investments.

Star M

LIZ

Hi Michelle,

LOVE IT LOVE IT LOVE IT................ You have done an awesome job of putting this together in such a relatable and non-judgmental way, congratulations! What I felt was warmth and understanding. I love the fact the book is conversational and doesn't 'preach' or 'lecture' the reader, as this is not what people want, I feel. People need help understanding and common sense advice that is easy to understand, and this is what you have provided.

Page 125 was excellent and explained just perfectly; I was nodding my head as I was reading.

For overall feel and content and ease of reading, I give you 10/10; it was magic. I would like to give you a personal testimonial if I may - do with it whatever you wish. "After filling our details into Bill Banisher, I was shocked to see how much my husband and I were going backwards each month. Our credit card was spiralling out of control, and I couldn't see a way to stop it; there never seemed to be enough money coming in. What was a bigger shock was the fact that I was the one handling the bill payments and I was also the 'spender'. Not a good combination, hence the credit card debt was my fault, so I needed to take responsibility for that. Bill Banisher has been a godsend to our household. We are now on track to eliminating our credit card debt and all of our bills are paid on or ahead of time - no more stress when a bill comes in.

The first couple of months were a little challenging, but it was necessary discomfort to be where we are now. We have learnt so much. This needs to be taught in our schools.

Thank you, Michelle, for giving us this freedom. -Liz

PS I will definitely recommend it to others.

CAROLYN

As the financial manager for our family, **I have tried and tested quite a few budgeting systems** over the past few years.

All of which have failed for some reason for other. So, when I was asked to read yet another book about budgeting, it seemed that this book would just be like all the others. Much **to my surprise, I thought I had struck gold** when from just reading I could tell straight away that this book would finally **address the problems I had with trying to make a budget actually work.**

What I liked most about the book was the step-by-step approach it takes to planning how one should approach managing your finances. Every step is clearly explained. No matter what your age group or financial situation, I believe this book can be of great benefit. Carolyn Murphy

ATHIL

I love Michelle's book "Financial Freedom on Your Current income" and the Bill Banisher System, because it teaches the foundations of money managing.

It is my belief that true financial wealth can only be reached once all our finances are in order, to a point where we no longer have to think about money. Thinking about it all the time implies that we do not have enough, which then creates our reality.

Bill Banisher allows me to be realistic about my lifestyle choices, so that I do not choose buying a car, only to find out that it causes me to get behind in my true-life dreams, which may have been to go on a holiday every year.

This system is different to the way I used to budget because the bank account systems controls your budget week by week, rather than spending your money and then seeing if you stuck to your budget. I recommend the Bill Banisher system to anybody who is serious about financial freedom, to be free from worrying if you have enough money for bills. Free from having to always miss out on things that are important, free from credit card debt, free from having money control me because now I control my money -- Athil Singh

TEPA

Hi Michelle...congrats on the book... Really enjoyed the practical and simple applications you have included in your book. They are principles that anyone and everyone can use.

You write from experience and not just an academic or theoretical perspective, which is evident in the content and easy-read style of your book. Anyone who picks this book up will be sure to take away with them firm financial principles to help them in life...good on you Michelle Tepa Faletoese

CHRISTOPHER

The greatest obstacle to financial freedom is NOT "learning how to make more money". I've seen people become finically free with an income of only a few hundred bucks a week. The greatest obstacle to financial freedom is... "not knowing how to handle your money as it flows in".

I've seen people make millions of dollars each year but never seem to be able to get 1themselves out of debt. Discovering how to handle your money is truly the greatest secret to

1

living an abundant life. In *Financial Freedom on Your Current Income*, Michelle hands you a simple plan to grow your money on autopilot – get it and begin living the extraordinary life you deserve to live! Christopher Guerriero, bestselling author and founder of Automatic Bestseller.

YOUR TESTIMONIAL GOES HERE!

2016 Revised and updated - Published by Strategeez Publishing Trust

2008 Published by Strategeez Publishing Trust
ACN 123 998 112
Po Box 421
Casula
NSW 2170

www.michellethmoneycoach.com

Ordering Information:

Quantity sales. Special discounts are available on quantity purchases by corporations, associations, and others. For details, contact the publisher at www.michellethmoneycoach.com.

DEDICATION

Dedicated to my awesome husband: without you, I cannot imagine my life. I thank the Lord every day for bringing you into my life.

To my beautiful children, who I hope to leave this legacy of good financial stewardship so that you won't have to learn the hard way, as we did.

To my favorite English teacher in high school, Mr. Robert Virgona, I only realized just as I put the finishing touches on this book what an impact you have had on my life. I was embarrassed the day you told the whole class that I reminded you of the young woman in the novel "My Brilliant Career" by Miles Franklin. It also just dawned on me; it was you who sparked in me the entrepreneurial spirit that has spurred me on through the years.

I pray that wherever you are, you are blessed. Thank you for your words of encouragement and that seed that has been buried deep inside me for the past thirty years.

The wonderful people I have had the pleasure of working with over the years in teaching this system, the people whose stories help me to help you.

And of course, to you, the person who reads this book looking to change your financial future; you are the reason I wrote this book.

ACKNOWLEDGEMENTS

Thanks to my awesome husband, who is the visionary, brains and the strategist in our partnership.

Not to mention, he is the best husband and father I could ever ask for. You are the wind beneath my wings. Thank you for believing in my dreams and always picking up the slack so that I could have the opportunity to pursue my dreams.

Thanks to my beautiful children, who always inspire me to be the best example I can be. I pray I can live up to most of your expectations. You of all people know how imperfect I am, and still love me.

Thanks to my wonderful friends Katherine, Helen, Toni and Lola, who gave their time, love and encouragement to make this vision a reality.

Yvonne and Keith (Mum and Dad), thank you for your transcription services, editing, babysitting and especially your encouragement. I appreciate that you always believe in me whatever I do, not only with your encouraging words, but also with your actions.

To all of my friends and family, too many to list, who encouraged me to get this book finished "because people need to hear this."

Who would have known it would be ready for a time such as this, October 2008, when all over the world people are hurting because of our Global credit crisis.

Now as I revise and update this book in 2016, the principles I teach have not changed. Some case studies have been added and some facts updated, and although there have been booms and busts both personally and as a society, the foundational principles remain the same. I am still managing my money the same way I have for over 16 years, and now my daughter has moved into her own apartment and has practiced these principles herself since her first pay check.

And, last but not least, thank you to my Heavenly Father, who planted the seed of a dream in my heart many years ago, and who has over the years held my hand through the tribulations that have in turn given me the wisdom to share with you in this book.

CONTENTS

INTRODUCTION

Have you ever found yourself thinking or even saying aloud…

> **"I make a pretty good income and we don't have a lavish lifestyle, so why is that we are worse off this year than we were last year and a year before that?"**

I'm pretty sure you have, because I've said it more than once myself in years gone by.

Have you ever wondered why you go to work every day, you bring home a decent income, and there never seems to be any left at the end of the month? There isn't enough money to go on holiday, there is nothing in your savings account for emergencies. And why is it that some people just seem to be able to do all of these things and never have a problem?

This is something that had me troubled for quite some time, and here are some observations I have made about this situation:

> ➤ It seems that 'cash flow' is called cash *flow* for a reason!
>
> Like a river, it needs to flow. If it does not have somewhere to flow to it will just flow out of your life.
>
> So, I have deduced that if you don't have a plan for where your money is going to go, it will end up in the pocket of someone else who does.
>
> For example, the person who owns the store that you buy all of those things that you don't really need from. Or

that partner of yours who spends any money available on toys, clothes or that new car that they absolutely have to have, reasoning that, after all, it's going to be much cheaper to run than the old one and it's only an extra couple of hundred dollars a month!

➢ When it comes to money problems, it is usually not the money that is the problem.

It is our attitude towards it, and until we change our attitudes we will never get rid of our money problems; they will just get bigger the bigger our income gets.

➢ If what we are doing now is not working, then we had better find a better way to do it, and keep finding out how to do it better until we succeed!

➢ Everything about the way we handle money, the way we spend money, and what we spend money on has changed. The old ways of managing money don't work anymore.

The challenge is no one is teaching us how to deal with the change, and some of us have not even realized that things have changed!

It breaks my heart to see people struggling just to make ends meet, let alone get ahead.

I have been helping people with this system on a one-on-one basis and in small groups for quite a while now; however, I really want to be able to help the whole community. That is why I have written this book.

I sincerely hope this book changes your life!

A word from Glen- I used to think if I could only make $100,000, then life would be easy. I could pay all my bills and life would be rosy. But you know what? You can be just as broke on $100,000 as you can be on $26,000 if you are spending more than you make, just as I was.

I had access to spreadsheets like VisiCalc and Lotus 123 way back in the 1980's, when IBM came out with its first IBM PC. I tried running a budget using a spreadsheet and I found that I could never get it to work! There was something missing in the formula. Something about human behavior; mine!

In 1995 I was working for Advance Bank, and they had the earliest internet banking product. So, I have also been using internet banking for a very long time. But even this didn't stop me from spending more than I earned.

It wasn't until the I.T. industry went into recession around 2001-2002, when I was out of work for the first time in my life and my income fell from $160k to $26k, that I actually had to work out how to budget properly.

I had read many books like The Richest Man in Babylon and many others, but I had not implemented any of the steps. Finally, I decided to work out how to implement the lessons in a practical way, so that we actually achieved a balanced budget, for the first time ever!

Not just balanced, but set up to prosper; there is a big difference between the two.

What I learned was that there are different types of people in the world. There are accounting type people who love analysing things. Nothing could be more exciting for them than to get themselves a café latté and a spreadsheet and work out what they spent last month…and then there's the rest of us.

There is one other thing I realized; when you budget the traditional way, you are looking at what happened, not what is going to happen…

I learned from my MBA that accountants have a secret. They use a technique called provisioning for depreciation, which means to provide for a future expense. When the average

3

person has their tax return done and they have something to depreciate, the accountant says, you have a tax deduction: 'free money from the Government', but what they don't tell you is, sooner or later you'll have a real expense coming up.

Large companies have always provisioned in their budgets. So why is it that the majority of us don't know we need to provision for depreciation in our own personal lives?

It's not your fault if you missed this little secret, because you are not the only one; it has only been in the last 10 years or so that our government started setting aside provisions in their budgets for replacing buildings and other things that wear out.

The fact is, it's not something that we learn about when we learn to manage our money.

Michelle is going to take you through the lessons we have learned from our own experiences, the multitude of books she has read as well as the experience of the people she has worked with over the past 16 years.

Please don't just skip to the end to find the answer, because if you do you will miss the important building blocks and insights that will help you to acknowledge why the current system is not working.

Before we discuss how to fix the problem, we first must understand what is causing us to fail.

As Dr Phil says, "You can't fix what you don't acknowledge."

WHY PEOPLE STILL STRUGGLE FROM PAYDAY TO PAYDAY, DESPITE THE ECONOMIC GOOD TIMES.

WE DON'T KNOW HOW TO USE THE CURRENT FINANCIAL SYSTEM TO OUR ADVANTAGE.

In the old days of cash, we divided our money into envelopes or jars and we saved up for things that we wanted; it was somewhat easier to live within our means, because when we ran out of money, that was it!

Nowadays, with credit cards, credit lines, and no further interest or payments for three years loans, we can keep spending, and most of us don't realize that we're spending $50, $200 or $300 a week more than what we're earning.

Hang on a minute, you say, my credit card is paid off at the end of every month. There is an automatic direct debit, attached to my credit line, that pays it off!

Most people who are using the line of credit loans with automatic direct debits paying out their balance have no idea that they are overspending. In fact, I have only ever met one person who "said" they could manage that type of loan, and they did it using spreadsheets and all sorts of fancy systems which 99% of people, including me, couldn't be bothered using.

What most of us don't understand is that this type of loan is actually set up to benefit the bank, not to benefit you. They want you to have more loans, so if you are overspending, that's fine; all that happens is your loan balance increases, and they make more money. And, worst of all, it is eating up the equity in your home and stealing your future wealth, and most of us don't even realize it!

What you will discover here is how to set up your finances to cost effectively use the current banking system to your advantage, which is totally opposite to what most banks want you to do.

We live in a fantastic time, as the use technology has improved the ease of managing our finances, and a few progressive banks have brought products onto the market that make it much easier for us to treat our money electronically as we used to when it was just cash. Now we find that most of the banks are trying to copy those accounts. However, most of them don't promote them heavily because they have to pay you much a higher interest rate, and there are a few catches that you need to watch out for that we will show you later in the book.

Using the banks to your own advantage will set you up to prosper, and not to create more debt. The second reason why people still struggle from payday to payday, despite the economic good times, is...

WE'VE LOST THE ABILITY TO "BUDGET TO GET AHEAD"

We buy now with the intention of paying later, and spend whatever comes in.

For some reason, when we do a budget we seem to budget to spend everything that comes in.

When I was in the public service and managing the budget for my area, I was told to make sure that the whole budget was spent, because if there was some left, I would get less to work with next year.

Now, I know that not everybody has worked for the public service. So, I just wonder where we get this notion of "using it all up" from.

Maybe it comes from being on diets; you know the old adage, "I'd better eat all of this stuff before I go on my diet." This attitude seeps through into our finances.

I prefer to use the term spending plan rather than budget, because a budget to me feels a bit like a diet; it restricts you, and you can really only stick to it for a short time.

What I want to show you is how to set up your spending plan on autopilot with a view to getting ahead financially, rather than just spending everything that comes in, and then some.

We are going to begin with the end in mind, rather than pay all the bills first and then do the important things like giving, investing and saving later. Which of course never happens, as we all know, after all the bills are paid there is usually nothing left, and we seem to live to that standard no matter what our income is.

Have you ever had a pay raise and thought, wow, now I can pay off that credit card or start to save some money, and found that the money was sucked up before you had chance to even start?

Have you also noticed that the opposite is true as well? Say you set up a payment plan and have money deducted to pay it; you only really miss it for a couple of weeks, and get used to not having it.

Some people think, "Oh, it's too restrictive to have a plan for where my money goes, I like to live for the moment. I work hard and I spend hard!"

That's all well and good if you could have total job security, which we all know is non-existent. If you think you are indispensable, just get injured and see how long it takes your boss to find someone to replace you. How do I know this? Because I've been there a few times!

Believe it or not, when you know where your money is going, it is actually very liberating rather than restricting, and you can get excited about the great things that you can achieve going forward.

Don't wait till you are thirsty to dig a well!!

If you practice the principles I am going to reveal to you, I know you will realize what I experience every day: **"Once you're ahead, you will never be behind again."** Instead of buying "stuff" that clutters your life, you can begin to get excited about buying assets that improve your life.

If you dig your well before you are thirsty, you will have a buffer against the third reason why people still struggle from payday to payday, despite the economic good times...

WE'RE NOT PREPARED FOR THE UNEXPECTED

How many times have you put into place a budget / spending plan, and five minutes after you implement it, something happens!

An unexpected car repair, or a large bill comes in, or the water heater breaks.

What do we do?

We put it on the credit card or even redraw on our line of credit loans, or we take the utility money to pay for it.

Until my dad started using the system that I'm about share with you, he used to say to me, oh it's a bad month this month, because I've got the car registration and the insurance due, as well as the electricity. All in one month!

Now I am not saying that because my dad is a strange person or anything like that. I think he is probably like just about every other person out there, except the accounting types who would never have this problem!

I was thinking about this one day. My dad has owned a car since he was about 20; he is now 60, so he has had a car for at least 40 years of his life and has been paying car registration and insurance every year for the past 40 years. So why is it such a big surprise that the car registration and insurance is due to be paid? He has also been paying electricity and gas bills, quarterly, for about the same amount of time. So why is receiving these bills so stressful, after all this time?

I have always thought that my dad is a pretty smart man. However, there seems to be something missing in the way he manages his money, which he hasn't recognized. Because for the past 40 years, he has been stressing about the same thing, and has not changed how he manages his money to fix the problem. I wonder if your parents have been doing the same, and so have you. I know I did!

So, let's begin by expecting the expected and the unexpected by provisioning for those things.

And by that I don't mean sticking the bills on the refrigerator or the calendar. I mean, actually planning for unexpected things like car repairs and fridges that need replacing and the expected large bills, like electricity and council rates/taxes. And putting money aside for it.

Now when the unexpected happens, you have the money for it already and it will be pretty much a non-event. How exciting is that? No more stress.

Just like me, you will be thinking, what on earth have I been doing all these years stressing over these ridiculous things?

Now you are ready for the fourth reason why people still struggle from payday to payday, despite the economic good times...

WE ARE FOREVER PLAYING CATCH UP, AND EVENTUALLY SOMETHING'S GOTTA GIVE!

We borrow for everything and spend 110% of what we earn.

Before we began using this system, I had a frequent-flier credit card, and I really got out of control with it; after all, with every dollar I spent I got a frequent-flier point. Woo hoo! I can go the Dubai business class and when I get back, I will spend the rest of my life paying it off.

What I did not understand at the time is, I was overspending by about $50 + a week.

$50 a week is not that much really, is it?

Well, it is about $2700 in a year! Therefore, I went from living within my means to having around $2700 of debt. Yuk!

Not to mention the interest that I was paying for that $2700. At about 16.25% interest, that is an extra $472 per year. Really yuk!

Interestingly enough, in 2007, I earned $500 of interest on the money that I spent!

Now that I have totally changed my spending habits, I am now earning that $500, rather than paying it interest. How exciting is that?

I still earn frequent flyer points on my card, but the balance is paid out every month and I still have practically the same available balance in my bank account, plus interest, that I had the previous month; it never goes below a certain level, even when I have a big month on my credit card. It works a bit like a money machine; as long as I don't spend more than I have allocated, it just keeps going around the machine and growing.

Why? Because everything is provisioned for.

It really doesn't take much to end up behind when you overspend on a credit card.

My first credit card, which I got when I was about 19, had a $500 limit, which I paid back at the end of every month, until…

I bought myself a new bed, which cost $150; this was the beginning of the end.

I couldn't pay it all out in the first month. I had a very low income and I didn't understand the effect of interest working against me. Then, a few months later was my boyfriend's 21st. Of course, I had to buy him a really nice gift. So, I spent about another $150 on that, and before I knew it that $500 credit card had $1000 of debt on it!

In those days, there were no over limit fees; if you did what I did today, those fees would just about wipe you out. I paid my card off in 1989 and was proud to be debt free. However, by 2002 it was maxed out again.

In 1992, I had an injury and was unable to work full time. As a single young woman with no family around, I still had to support myself without my full income. So, I paid the minimum payment each month for about 2 years, and by that time I was in the same amount of debt as when I started out.

You can see from these examples that if you don't change the habit, it can take ages to even get back to zero. Then a minute to get right back on the merry go 'round!

WHY ARE WE STILL SPINNING OUR WHEELS OR, WORSE, DROWNING IN DEBT?

UNDERSTAND WHY "QUICK FIX" SOLUTIONS ARE A MYTH, AND WON'T GET YOU OUT OF DEBT.

Before I show you what works, let's look at the things we do that don't work.

BURY YOUR HEAD IN THE SAND

If you don't think you are good at managing finances, or you're too scared or lazy to do it, then you can do what a lot of people I have worked with do. Let your partner handle it.

The big catch is, do they know what they are doing any better than you would?

In many cases, the answer is no!

I was talking to a young woman the other day about what her parents taught her about managing her money when she was young. This is what she said…

"My mum taught me that I should get a job while I was at school and earn some money; she put some of the money away in a savings account and gave the rest to me when I needed it. So, I guess she taught me that I should save money, but I don't really know why. And the rest of it she did for me."

I said OK, so your mum managed your money for you, until you moved in with your fiancé, and then what happened?

"I gave it to him to manage; he looks after all the money." Regardless of whether or not he was doing a good job of managing the money. You can see from the story that most the time, we just do what we were "taught" or saw happening around us when we were young. Unless we realize we need help from somebody else along the way, most of us don't really know what we are doing.

In my own case, I moved out of home at 16 and earned a very low income: $65.04, to be exact. Isn't it funny how you never forget how much you earned in your first job?

My parents always seemed to struggle with money, and I remember mum stressing about the bills. My dad always liked to buy "toys"; power tools, car parts, etc., which of course were all necessities.

I don't remember being taught at home about saving money, although I had a school bank account that mum would give me 50 cents to put in every month. Back then, the schools had a program where the banks came and set up bank accounts for the children and taught them about having a savings account; I am not sure that they even do that anymore.

I was taught that I needed to pay board, so as soon as I was working I paid $20 a week, which my parents gave back to me when I moved out of home to pay my bond for the group house that I lived in.

By the time I paid my rent, food and utilities, there was $10 a week left, so I used to say, "I don't have any money to save."

What I know now is that I should have been putting one or two dollars a week away regardless. The habit alone would have totally changed my future relationship with money.

So, as I think about these stories, and about people who I've worked with, I realized that there are a lot of people who live life this way; they just leave it all up to their partner and don't really know what's going on. To me that's a pretty dangerous predicament to be in, because if the other person is doing a bad job, you could be falling into a very deep hole and not know about it until it's too late, which I have seen many times.

With a divorce rate around 50%, we all need to take responsibility for our finances, especially if you are a woman with children, and not take a chance on letting our partner handle it all, burying our head in the sand and not knowing where the money is going. We all need to have at least an account or two in our own name so that we can build up our own credit rating, as well as experience at managing the finances; you never know what is around the corner.

I have seen so many capable and intelligent people end up in a whole lot of trouble with this style of money management.

If I'm talking about you right now, the great thing is it's really not rocket science.

You can do it!

The next wheel spinning, debt-creating quick fix myth is the...

Fudge-it Budget

We've all been on a 'diet' that failed and we've all had some kind of budget that failed as well.

Most of us have been using some kind of a budget; some are formal, others are informal.

Some of us just have it in our head, keep spending until we get into trouble and clean up the mess after it happens.

If you've ever applied for a loan, what's the first thing that the bank gets you to do?

A budget.

I call this a fudge-it budget.

It's the budget you do when you work all your expenses out in such a way that it looks like you can afford the loan that you are applying for, even though you really can't.

How do I know about this? Because I've done it!

I have a friend who has always struggled financially. When she wants something new, she will say to me, "It's only another $20 a month, I can afford that!"

The challenge is that she really can't afford it.

Where the trouble begins is when you add up $20 a month here and $20 a month there. It doesn't take long to be spending an extra hundred dollars a month, which, when you're on a very low income, can really get you into a lot of trouble.

Not to mention the fact that you will never actually catch up; you are always behind.

I know what you are thinking! I earn a good income. I can actually afford the extra $100 a month!

The thing is, if you can afford the extra hundred, you will probably spend an extra $300, because your lifestyle will be relative to your income. So, it doesn't matter whether you earn $20,000 or $120,000 if you manage your money in this style. You will be forever playing catch up.

It really comes down to changing your habits and avoiding the next wheel spinning, debt-creating quick fix myth, the....

CONSOLIDATION CON JOB

Consolidating your debt can be a great option, if you have several loans with high interest rates and you need to get your finances under control.

The problem is that usually what happens after debt consolidation paperwork is signed and the loans are cleared, there comes another spending spree!

Woo-hoo, that was fun, now let's pay it off again!

It's not necessarily the debt consolidation that is the problem; it is the fact that most of the time, the habits have not changed. Once the debts are *moved,* you can "feel free of the burden", which can sometimes lull you into a false feeling of prosperity, ending up with thought patterns like this: "It's ok to buy this," or, "It's only $20 a month and we can afford it now." Woops, here we go again, out of control. When you consolidate, the debts are not paid off; they are moved to a different type of loan, and the payments are reduced because the debt is spread out over a longer period. If you don't manage this properly, you can end up in even more debt for a longer time, costing you much more in the long run.

If you cut the credit cards up, or at the very least put them somewhere where you cannot use them, this can be a successful option as long as you set up a way to pay the debt down. I will discuss this further later in the book.

You must, however, be very conscious of what type of consolidation loan you get. If you have a property, the type of loan that you often end up with is one where you deposit all of your income into the account and have a credit card, which is paid off at the end of each month using a direct debit attached to a line of credit loan on your house. I have only met **one** person who says they can successfully manage this type of loan.

I know you are thinking, isn't paying my credit card at the end of the month a good thing? Of course, it is. However, if you look at the way the cash flows, that system is actually set to benefit the bank, not you. If you overspend without realizing, it just eats up your equity and you end up further in debt.

That's great for the bank, not you!

The habit must change, or you will end up right where you started.

Some friends came into a large amount of money. They didn't go on a spending spree. Instead, they spent an extra $100 a week and had a holiday here and a holiday there. Five years later, and there is none left!

If you spend all that you earn, you will be exactly where you are now, less depreciation!

Now for the other popular money management, wheel spinning, stress-and-debt-creating quick fix myth…

ROB PETER TO PAY PAUL

This is the method of budgeting I used to use when I was single.

I would write rubber checks, and then shuffle the money to cover it. A rubber check is a check written when there are no funds in the bank to cover it, resulting in a bounced check if it is presented before the money is shuffled; an expensive system when it fails.

I used a "sweat it card." That's the card that is $500 over its limit, then you stand at the checkout sweating over whether they will decline it or not.

This is a very stressful way to live, and impossible to manage if you are a couple.

I met a man recently who was long term unemployed and had $20,000 of credit card debt with an interest rate of 18%. He came to me when I was volunteering at a charity for people in financial difficulty. I told him that he should immediately see a financial counselor because he really needed to 'stop the bleeding.'

He said he couldn't because they would make him get rid of the new credit card he had just received, as he was using it to pay the minimum payment on the other cards!

No doubt, he now has $24,000 of debt and is still looking for free food coupons.

This is a very stressful way to live, because you are always scraping the bottom of the barrel to pay whichever bill is more urgent…always…always…

The other thing that I have seen people do is start saving for a utility bill, but when something else comes up, they spend it on that instead.

I have also seen many cases where a couple uses a joint account with about $1000 in it. All of a sudden, the partner, usually **not** the person who pays the bills, says I 'need' a new TV, golf clubs, or something, and there is sudden amnesia that there is a $750 electricity bill just days away!

If you are in this situation in your relationship, then it's a really good idea to have separate bank accounts!

The other important thing would be to sit down together, face your situation, and change the habits now.

Hopefully you have seen some of the myths working in your life right now and are keen to move forward to a future where these are not myths you will buy into again.

IT'S NOT YOUR FAULT...
WHY WE END UP REPEATING THE SAME
BAD HABITS OVER AND OVER AGAIN,
DESPITE OUR BEST INTENTIONS.

DIDN'T YOUR PARENTS TEACH YOU?

Our parents don't know how to manage their money using the current banking system, so how can they teach us?

I know this because we have taught my parents to use this system.

In fact, even though we have been using internet banking etc. since its inception, we still couldn't figure out how to make it "work for us" until we had to.

I was talking to one of my mom's friends about this and she agreed, and then told me how she manages her money.

"I write down everything I spend on my card in a book at the end of the day, and then I know where I'm at and have no surprises when the bill comes in."

I congratulated her and told her she was 1 in a million; in my experience that system does not work long term, especially with two people using one credit card or check book. Not to mention the hassle of having to remember to write it all down!

You can tell I have tried these ideas before and FAILED! Maybe we youngsters (in our 40's) are lazy and undisciplined.

If you are a single person, using just a credit card or checking account, it "could" work for a very self-disciplined person, but throw a partner into the mix, not to mention one who is undisciplined and a spender, and you have fireworks!

How many times have you heard couples complaining about their partner not writing an expense down in the check book?

Once again, it is the system that has changed, but we are still trying to use it to do things the way we always have in the past.

THE PAY RAISE DELUSION

We say, as soon as I get that pay raise, we will get ahead!

When we get one, somehow it just gets sucked up, and we are worse off than before.

I remember once I got a pay raise and ended up with 50 cents a week less than I was getting before! Huh!

It turned out that I was now in a higher tax bracket, and then there was the superannuation, and some other deduction.

The fact is, if you are spending it all now, you will spend it all then.

Because you have not changed your habits!

How do I know?

Personal experience. I used to say the same thing when I was earning $17,000, then $25,000 and even $120,000.

We were just as "broke" on $160,000 as we were on $40,000.

If you cannot manage your money when you earn a small income, how can you manage a large income?

As Dr. Phil says, money problems are not necessarily money problems. Most of the time, they are just the manifestation of priority and attitude problems.

I see it every day when people come to me for help with their finances.

When our income fell from $160,000 to $26,000 we had to change our priorities big time. And you know what? We did not starve or go without anything we "needed."

INTEREST IGNORANCE TRAP

We have worked with people in our budgeting workshops with credit card bills of $25,000 and, in some cases, much more.

They had consumed whatever it was that they had bought and are now hit with an interest bill of $416 every month. Unless things change, they will have that debt until the day they die.

In fact, did you know that these people are paying for someone else's money tree? I will talk about the money tree later in the book.

What is the interest ignorance trap?

If there is any residual debt on a purchase of something that is consumed, you will enter into an interest ignorance trap.

For example, when you purchase food and gas on a credit card, it is consumed; there is nothing left to show for the bill you have, and there is nothing to sell if you needed to liquidate.

The lure of an emotional purchase tempts us to spend money that we cannot afford. This attraction can trap you forever in a never-ending cycle of debt.

LET ME GIVE YOU TWO EXAMPLES: JANE AND MICHAEL

Jane goes down to the shops and sees a beautiful red dress. It costs $279, and she cannot afford it.

Every time she goes shopping, she sees it in the window and she wants it. Weeks pass, and there is a special on in the store. The dress is marked down to $179. That's a $100 saving. She still cannot afford it, but she puts it on her credit card and now owes $179 on her card.

The Card Company only requires her to pay 3% of the balance

each month, so she pays $5.37 per month for her dress. Not very expensive – right?

Jane has a dress that she values at $279 for $5.37. If Jane just makes the minimum payments, how long does it take her to pay it off?

After 3 years, Jane still owes $113.00 on the dress and has paid $83.00 in interest, and it still has not been paid off. In fact, if Jane keeps paying the bare minimum, she still owes money after 6 years.

The credit card company counts on Jane being in perpetual debt, because after 6 years the dress has now cost her another $137, making the cost of the dress $316; she still owes $79. After 6 years, the dress will probably be discarded, but the $70 debt remains. It is not the fact that Jane purchased the dress that is the problem; the problem is that she could not promptly pay off the whole amount for the dress. She could not afford the dress, full stop!

Michael has an unreliable car. He has no savings. Every day he drives down the road and there are many new and used car lots on his way to work.

Michael spots a car he likes the look of, and every day as he drives past he dreams a bit about driving down the road in that brand-new car.

Finally, one day, he pulls into the car lot. The ticket price was $32,000. Before you know it, Michael has signed a $25,000 loan for a new car after trading in his old car for $7000.

You see, emotionally he had already bought it in his mind weeks ago. Michael signs up for an interest rate of 14.75%. Everyone knows that the car lots mark up their cars a bit.

As it turns out, he could have bought the same car at auction for $19,000 or privately for $26,000. He pays the car off at $703 per month over 4 years, but how much does it cost him?

The car worth about $26,000 cost him an additional $8,000 to buy and a further $8069 in interest payments over the 4 years.

Cars generally depreciate by 10% a year, so after 4 years the car is now approximately 40% less than when purchased.

Therefore, when he finally pays off the car, it's worth about $15,000, or maybe a bit less. Would you buy a car that is worth $26,000 for $40,000? Including finance, that is exactly what Michael did. In this scenario, Michael's cost of ownership (not including taxes, registration or insurance) is $25,000, or $6,250 a year.

You see, if Michael had a good credit rating and planned his purchase in advance, perhaps he could have secured an interest rate of around 8%. If he planned to buy the car at auction, he could have purchased the car for $19,000.

If Michael had done this, his interest cost would have been $3,194 and his monthly payment $472. He would be $231 per month better off. In this case, Michael would have bought a car for $22,194 that after 4 years is worth $15,000. In this instance, Michael's cost of ownership is $7,194, or $1,798 per year. A saving of $4,452 a year, or $85 per week better off.

There is still debate as to whether or not a car should be financed at all, and there are arguments on both sides of the coin. The main point I want to make here, however, is that credit companies can easily take advantage of you when you enter into a credit agreement for something that has a high emotional content, especially if it depreciates over time.

If you think you can afford $703 per month for a replacement car, then why not start saving that amount of money in a high-interest, zero-fee savings account for at least 3 or 4 months to make sure you can really afford the cost? However, it may be more important to crunch the numbers and spend a little time doing some research before you go ahead.

Most importantly, make sure that you can pay off all of your consumer debt promptly. Preferably at the end of each month, if it is a credit card.

WE DON'T KNOW ANY BETTER

The teachers don't know how! Most of the bankers don't know how, either!

More money won't fix the problem, and neither will another budget.

It took a drop from $160,000 to $26,000 to get us to get our attitudes and principles right and make our money work for us, instead of being slaves to it.

I have been speaking with CEO's in the banking industry, and they say to me:

"You know, I think I even need to do your course."

What does that tell you? Most of the people working in the banks don't know any better than the rest of us!

The banking system, the way we are paid, the ease of borrowing money, etc., have all changed so much over the past 20 years that only a very few people have managed to keep up with it.

The rest of us just keep doing what we are doing, because it is too hard to figure out:

• Which bank is best for us

• What type of account to use -Savings account, credit card, debit card, personal loan, car loan or mortgage

• How to avoid the fees

On top of all of the other decisions that we have to make every day, like:

• Which phone package

• Which Internet company

• What is the best cell phone plan

I know people who use banks that have shocking customer service, pay low interest rates on savings and charge exorbitant fees on the money invested. They stay with that company because they feel like it's just too hard to swap.

It is time for us to get wise. There is now so much information available on the internet; there are even web sites that compare bank accounts, credit cards, phone plans and just about anything you want to compare.

Why not set aside some time and do a little research and planning in your financial life? I'm sure you can save yourself a fortune if you do. I know I have.

Did you know that most people spend more time planning a vacation than they spend on planning their financial future?

No wonder we are spinning our wheels!

In the next chapter, I'm going to give you the biggest reasons why we are failing financially. There are several reasons, and the number one reason is not what you might think.

BUDGETS
WE HAVE A BOOKSHELF FULL OF BUDGETING BOOKS.

THE NUMBER ONE REASON WHY
BUDGETS DON'T WORK…

DE FACTO FINANCES

The biggest reason, in my experience, for the failure of budgets is de facto finances.

In all of the budgeting books and systems I have looked at, I have not seen anyone else talk about this missing piece of the budgeting puzzle.

When we do our budget on a spreadsheet, in a book, or on a web site, it does not translate to the reality of our bank accounts and the flow of our cash.

The money is in the account, or should I say the credit is available on the card, and the budget sits on the fridge or computer, and the budget Is not connected to them; they are not married.

No matter what medium you use to plan your spending, if it's not married to the actual money that comes in and out of your bank account, "the cash flow", it won't work long term.

We live in a wonderful time when, finally, the banks are

beginning to catch on and develop banking products that suit our needs, thanks to the influence of progressive organizations like ING Direct. However, often the bank's staff does not really know how to use them effectively, let alone teach us how to use them.

The system that we use solves the problem of backward budgeting and de facto finances and sets you up with a plan to prosper, all by using the banking system to your advantage and simplifying your life.

LACK OF SELF DISCIPLINE

The next big one of the top four reasons why conventional budgets fail is lack of self-discipline.

Now I'm not saying that we are all totally undisciplined, although some of us might be and I would include myself in this basket. Who can get excited about coming home, sitting down with a spreadsheet and tracking everything you spend for the rest of your life? Not me!!! For starters, you are really only accounting for what has happened in the past; it's over, you can't change it, and it doesn't stop you from overspending.

Have you noticed that the average budget has a projected column and an actual column? If the budget worked, you would be pretty much on target, and not have to worry about filling that column in anyway!

If you are anything like me, I find it time-consuming and downright boring to sit down and work out what I spend every week and enter it into the spreadsheet.

And let's face it, if most of us have self-discipline problems, we won't do it anyway.

I find it hard to get up and go to the gym; I have things on my to-do lists, but I just don't do them.

So if you are not super self-disciplined like me, you are the reason why I wrote this book. You are the average person, like me, who wants to get a handle on this and stop spinning your wheels and feeling like a failure, as I did.

Let me just put one caveat on the previous chapter, and that is, if you are out of control in your spending, you should actually track your spending for a little while, just to find out where you're at. But once you've done that, you really should not have to do that again, if you are using the system that I am sharing with you.

SPENDING PERSONALITY

There is quite a bit of information about personality types and a stack of different methods of describing them. Just Google the term "spending personality" and you can find a multitude of labels to define yourself with. So, I won't go into it too much here

Regardless of which "system" you subscribe to, we all have a personality type.

Most of us can easily figure out what ours is.

I'm sure you've heard the saying "opposites attract"; in my experience, I would say amen!

I usually see a manager and a saver or a manger and a spender in a relationship; it makes for a little excitement in their lives.

God forbid if you have two spenders together, as they are usually the ones on Oprah or Dr. Phil getting a financial makeover!

The thing that usually causes friction in relationships is if their "personality" is out of control.

What I mean by that is if the spender is spending out of control, or the manager is over managing, or the saver is leaning to the tightwad end of the scale and is sucking the fun out of life. There needs to be some balance brought back into the financial relationship, or there might be some problems brewing in other areas of the relationship.

There is hope for all of us regardless of our spending personality because, believe it or not, we are all in control of our personality. We can bring our habits back into balance and have harmony in our lives.

Once you admit to the areas where you are out of control, you can then begin to change and be in charge of your spending, instead of your spending being in charge of you.

I am guilty of being a spender, and if I can get my spending under control, so can you. I have actually changed my spending personality from spender to saver/spender. I now save money to buy an asset, which gives me more money to spend; a perfect situation for a spender. Now I am what Loral Langemeier, the millionaire-maker, calls an asset addict. I have just changed what I spend my money on to something that builds wealth rather than eating it up.

FINANCIAL ESPIONAGE

As we talk about budgeting with people, unfortunately we have started to uncover some of the sneaky and dirty things that partners will do to each other financially.

I think that men in particular are more embarrassed about their financial impotence than anything else, and often will not talk about it with their partners.

A friend came out of the hospital with a newborn baby to find the phone had been disconnected. In addition, two days later she received an electricity disconnection letter. The frightening thing about it is that the husband and wife had not discussed what happened! This is an absolute disaster because of the flow-on effects in the relationship.

I coined the phrase 'financial espionage' to describe how one partner undermines the other financially. When men are in trouble financially, they often start doing overtime to try to cover the shortfall, but usually they just don't understand the real problem. Often, the reason the finances are out of control is not financial.

Then the wife, lacking attention because he is never home,

buys things they can't afford; often it is clothing, or things for the children.

He gets angry at her, then goes and buys a case of beer or, even worse, a new car that they cannot afford.

Would you fix a leak in the bath by just running the tap faster? I don't think so.

Financial espionage, as the term suggests, is a sneaky way to undermine the other partner financially. I call it espionage because it is covert. So, one partner might set up a budget and the other partner simply ignores it or incurs a debt secretly. One partner 'forgets' to pay bills or uses money allocated for bills for other things. A partner is always saying how he/she 'really needs' this or that – everything is always a necessity.

Or on the other extreme of the spectrum, a partner is made to account for every cent, while the other is accountable for nothing. This is a way for a dominant partner to control the other and try to prove the other is 'wrong'.

Financial espionage is very difficult to deal with. Firstly, the offending partner will deny that it is happening. As soon as you approach them, the blame is instantly turned onto you. Even if you get past that hurdle, your partner will then use plausible deniability, like "I didn't know."

There has to be an agreed set of rules that both partners will play by.

If there are serious problems in your relationship in this area, it would be a good idea to involve a professional counsellor in the process.

The only way out is to sit down with the facts and discuss a way to move forward.

By using technology to your advantage, it can be a lot easier to control this behaviour without constant confrontation.

How do you resolve financial espionage?

1. A certain amount of money must be set aside into a separate account to pay for bills.

2. Partners have a card account of their own and a certain amount of money they are **NOT** accountable for; let's say 2.5% of the weekly net income, for example.

3. Each partner is responsible for paying some of the bills.

4. Apart from a medical emergency, one partner should not bail out the mistakes of the other once this is set up, otherwise the espionage will continue indefinitely. This point is conditional on the fact that the mistakes are not due to not having enough to work with in the beginning.

For example, I had a client whose partner had never given her enough money to cover the expenses she was responsible for.

In this case, it is no wonder she was stressed and suffering depression. Her partner would constantly tell her she just needed to budget better. Which she believed until we put their real numbers into Bill Banisher; then the lights came on.

She was able to prove to him that it was not all her fault. No one could have made her finances work.

In this example, it is obvious that there are also underlying problems in the relationship; lack of communication, understanding and empathy. In a situation like this marriage, counselling is also necessary. The financial problems were the manifestation of other problems in the relationship.

I am pleased to say that using the Bill Banisher system was an important step in the positive outcome in this situation.

FINANCIAL INFIDELITY

Financial infidelity is another big issue in the area of financial espionage.

Financial infidelity is where you buy things, for example, a dress, you take the tags off, put it in the wardrobe and you bring it out 6 months later. When you wear it, your husband says, "Oh, is that a new dress?" and you say, "Oh no, I have had it for ages." Technically, you are telling the truth, because you have had it for ages. However, deep down you know you are lying.

It's not just women who are guilty of this. Men do it too, however, I hear about this one mostly from women. Probably because they feel they can admit it to another woman without fear.

It could just as easily be buying things on eBay, or anywhere else for that matter. Or using a credit card that your partner does not know about.

I have worked with quite a few people who have credit cards with substantial balances on them that their partner does not even know they have.

If you have been involved in this activity, it's time to fess up and begin the healing process. Holding onto that kind of stress can cause you illness in the long term, not to mention the tension it will create in your relationship.

I would not have to even bother to engage in this behaviour, because Glen is one of those people who doesn't notice those little things, like a change in hair color; even if I change it to purple. I am always jibing him about it.

There are, however, some advantages to his lack of notice; when I am complaining about how messy the house is because it looks like a bomb went off, he says, "What mess? It looks fine to me!"

My son James would catch me, however. A few months ago, I bought some new shirts. I got dressed to go out and my 9-year-old son James said, "Wow, Mommy, that shirt looks great. Is that a new shirt? I haven't seen you wear it before."

Glen was standing nearby; he sidled up to me and whispered, "Is it new?"

I said it sure is! He just shrugged his shoulders and looked rather embarrassed.

SEXUALLY TRANSMITTED DEBT

On the subject of marriage, one of the worst STD's you could get is sexually transmitted debt. That is where (from couples I've seen, it's often the husband) comes into the relationship smelling like roses but soon after the marriage it becomes apparent that the show is a house of cards, and the financially successful partner ends up bailing out the others debts; however, as quickly as they fix up one thing, there is another.

These men are usually very, very charming, and the woman applies – let's call it "magical thinking" to the situation. I.e. if I just fix this, then everything will be ok. There are usually warning signs before they even walk down the aisle, however the magical thinking helps them stay in denial until the house of cards comes tumbling down.

A word of warning: In every one of this type of case I have come across, the charming partner is a serial offender.

Be aware when old friends and past girlfriends say, "Watch out for your credit card."

I'm not saying that every interpersonal risk can be mitigated, but a husband and wife (de facto or formal) must be able to discuss and negotiate finances without getting into a fight or a stalemate.

Glen and I sit down together and write up our personal and shared goals for the coming few years, then work out how to fund them, using our money or other peoples' money (for investments), whatever the case may be. Our kids are involved in the goal setting as well and if they want to be, they are involved in our financial discussions.

They will need to know how to handle these conversations in their own relationships one day; why not let them see how it is done first hand?

Sexually transmitted debt is becoming more and more prevalent as the population ages and the divorce rate climbs. This STD is not limited to the bedroom, though, as the name suggests. We can get it from our children.

There is a phenomenon called Boomerang children. This is adult children coming home to live with mom and dad after divorce or a job loss and never leaving, often bringing children with them. There is absolutely nothing wrong with coming home for help to get back on your feet. Where the problem lies is when the child doesn't get back on their feet and mooches off the parents, causing them to have financial difficulties themselves.

Divorce is also making a huge number of men and women carriers of STD into their new relationships. It is really important to get financially naked with your partner before you actually get into bed with them, so to speak. If you can't get financially naked with your partner, then don't bother with the other; it will only lead to bigger problems down the track.

Knowing your partner's expectations and beliefs around money is one of the most important things to get right before you move into a committed relationship. Sexually transmitted debt is not terminal, but it can take a long time to clear up and cause both of you trouble and stress.

THE 5 STEPS
TO FINANCIAL HEALTH...

THE FULL STORY

I can't remember exactly what the dates were, but this is how the scenario went.

Sometime during 2001, the IT industry just crashed. Several very large public companies went under and suddenly there were hundreds of very highly qualified Information Technology specialists out of work. There was fall out in all sections of the industry.

The project Glen was working on was completed, and he was on the market for another job.

Every time Glen went into the market, he would be out of work for a maximum of two weeks, he would usually be offered a couple of jobs, and his interview strike rate was 1 in 2. We have never been concerned about him being out of work, until then.

He had never applied for unemployment benefits in his whole life.

Because we fully expected him to find work any day, we did not apply for unemployment benefits immediately because we did not think we would need it.

We waited for over two months to apply, and when we did, they said we did not qualify. Because we had cash in our company.

We had borrowed equity from our home to invest, which had

come through about two weeks before Glen was given notice to finish his contract. The unemployment office told us we would have to use all of the money to live on, before we would qualify.

We had been paying our taxes at the highest rate for years and when we needed help, it was not available.

I was furious; they wanted us to live on money that was borrowed. As you know by now, that is totally against my principles.

The money was not even ours, technically, anyway; it belonged to our company, which is essentially as if it belonged to another person. Legally, it was not ours to use for that purpose.

That money was the debt we had to pay back when he finally did work again.

Glen finally found work after 3 months, at a significantly lower rate than his previous contract.

We put a debt repayment system in place and set up the system we are sharing in this book.

We were never going to allow ourselves to be in a situation like that again. We wanted to be prepared for an emergency such as that.

Six months later, about a week after we had finished paying back the debt from the previous three months of unemployment, Glen was told that the job was done and he would not have his contract renewed.

Can you imagine how that would feel, especially when we knew the employment situation was even worse than before?

It was a scary thought; however, we felt that we were prepared.

We had been practicing what we preached for six months.

We had six months of 10% saving and 10% investing in the bank.

We felt very confident, and we had enough to keep us going for about four months without any stress. We had no debt, and all of our payments were at least 3 months in advance.

When three months passed without even one call for an

interview, we were getting low on funds and we thought we had better go apply for unemployment benefits.

It took another seven weeks for them to determine whether we qualified. Because we have a company, it makes it more complicated to assess.

By this time, we were down to our last $200, and I began to be a little worried.

We did, however, have faith that our prayers and the prayers of our friends who were praying for us would be answered.

I also knew from previous experience that God has a sense of humor, and he likes to make us wait until the eleventh hour just so we know he is involved in the outcome.

The next week, the money came in.

Let me just give you some statistics about Glen's job hunting. When he was out of work, his full-time job was to find work. He applied for about seven jobs a day at least, often more. We stopped counting after he had applied for 400 jobs in 3 months without even a call back.

By this time, he was even applying for laboring jobs, which he did not even get a look in, because they considered him over qualified.

He began to take many of his qualifications out of his resume, hoping to get any kind of work.

I hope you can see he is an amazing man. He was not a snob about what he was prepared to do, and the thing I am proudest of is that through all of this, he only got down in the dumps for one day, when this had been going on for 12 months!

I cannot say it was the same for me. I was not always a happy camper!

While we were on unemployment benefits, we still practiced these principles. It was very difficult, and we had to say no to a lot of things the children asked for.

Of course, we did not do the full 10%; it was more like 5%, 5%,

7%. That equated to a few dollars per week, but at least it was something.

When we got through those 14 months, I felt proud of the fact that we had kept our family happily together with minimal stress over money. And most importantly, we did not have a bill that we could not pay during that time, even though we had a $300k mortgage and three very small children.

I even had about $500 in my investing account.

That is why I can say to you that you can do this on any income. It is just a matter of getting your priorities in the right place.

In the next chapter, I will show exactly how we managed to move through that difficult time and not have a bill that we could not pay, while people all around us lost marriages, self-respect and their possessions.

STEP ONE
UNDERSTAND THE "UNIVERSAL" LAWS OF MONEY

PRINCIPLE OF GIVING

Giving or blessing others is great for your self-esteem and for your finances.

This is a universal principle, and it works no matter what your creed!

"I have found that while my hands are out to bless other people, I am always blessed far beyond what I can give away."

The worst thing that can happen is you will feel good about helping someone else.

A good place to start is to bless organizations that have blessed you.

For example, "Many years ago, when I was out of work and flat broke, I received a few food parcels from The Smith family charity. I am always happy to give to them because they have helped me and I know they really make a difference."

You could sponsor a child.

Child sponsorship is a great way to inspire your children to be compassionate about the needs of others.

We give to our local church, the local community radio station we listen to, sponsor a child and contribute weekly to help a friend who is going through a tough time at the moment.

We also have a "giving account" which is used for giving "seed money" to start something worthwhile; or to give to worthy causes over and above the ones mentioned above.

> For example, to encourage a friend with a fantastic voice, we paid to have a song recorded for her album. It helped her in several ways, some we had no idea about until after we did it.

1. It helped her have faith that she could succeed, because we were willing to put our money behind her. She was encouraged that someone other than her mother believed she had a voice that needed to be heard, and was willing to put, what she perceived as a lot of money, towards achieving her dream.

2. It inspired others. When other people heard that someone else was willing to put money toward the project, people came out of the woodwork and offered help, doing artwork for free, and the band volunteered to play free. In addition, people who were too busy to help previously suddenly had time to help.

3. It gave her insight into how a limiting mindset can hold you back. Sometimes we think the barrier we are facing is huge, but to someone else it is nothing; in this case, the amount of money she was held back by was miniscule to me, but to her it seemed so big. She now sees the situation differently.

4. It made us feel good to be helping someone we love and believe in take a step towards achieving their dreams.

How many times have you heard about a cause and you think, "Wow, that is fantastic, I wish I had some money to help." We used to say that to ourselves before we set up our finances in such a way that there is always some to give first.

We believe so strongly in giving back that we have set up a charitable Not for Profit with a goal to teaching financial literacy in schools and in the community.

There are so many worthy causes out there.

Find something you believe in and back them.

IF YOU CAN'T GIVE MONEY, THEN GIVE YOUR TIME.

Have you ever noticed that people who are so attached to their money that they have trouble with giving it are often the very people who seem to always be worried about money?

I believe that giving is a necessity in our spending plan.

I need to give not because God "needs" my money to make miracles happen, but because I need to have a giving attitude. It also makes me unattached to money and things, and guess what? Miracles do happen because we give.

Why don't you give it a try!

Now it's a free world, and if I have not been able to convince you that giving is a necessity and this is something you don't want to do, then put the giving 10% towards debt reduction, saving and investing.

At the very least, you may be inspired to help someone one day, and you will have some money to use.

Don't just spend it!

BUILD WEALTH WITH YOUR MONEY TREE

INVESTING

Have you ever heard the saying, "You have to pay yourself first"?

I hear it all the time from financial planners and other people in the finance industry.

Does anyone actually know what that means, and, more importantly, how to do it? No, most people have no idea. This one certainly had me confused for about 10 years.

I learned the invest 10% principle, also known as the pay yourself first principle, about thirty years ago, and actually put away 10% of my income for about 10 years, but I did not know what investing actually was.

Maybe you can relate. I know most people I talk to are also confused.

I thought it meant save up and spend it on things I want like holidays, jewellery or a new car!

Now that I know what it is, it makes me sick to think of how much further ahead I would be financially if I had truly understood what investing really was thirty years ago.

Investing is very important for the long and short term, because It is how you grow yourself a money tree.

The money tree produces money for you that you do not have to trade hours for dollars to earn; passive income. It makes money while you sleep to grow your wealth or net worth, and it is there to fall back on in times of trouble.

My favourite Bible story is about Joseph.

Remember how his brothers hated him because he had a

dream about being in charge of them? So they sold him as a slave.

I love Joseph because he was a man with a vision, as well as a man of character. Many bad things happened to him, and he even went to jail for something he did not do. Joseph never felt sorry for himself; he held onto his dream and practiced the principles he was taught by his father, who loved him.

He ended up in charge of the jail and eventually was in charge of the whole country of Egypt.

There was a great famine, and he was responsible for feeding the starving people of the surrounding nations.

I know what you are thinking! What do Joseph and the famine have to do with investing?

A lot!

Joseph's story teaches us:

1. You have to have a vision.

2. You have to believe you can achieve it.

3. You have to provision for it financially.

You see, if the Egyptians under his rule did not provision for the famine, they would not have had any extra food to last the famine themselves, or to feed the other nations.

You might be thinking:

- I know nothing about investing

- I don't want to learn about it either

- I'm not smart enough

- You have to have a lot of money to invest

- My partner handles all of the money stuff

What I want you to know for sure is:

There is a famine coming at some time in your life. Whether it is a period of unemployment or an injury, it will be something totally out of your control, and if you have no provisions, you will starve.

The truth is a big tree starts out as a small seed; if you begin to invest a small amount over a long time and let compound interest work in your favour, you will grow a large money tree.

One of the biggest excuses I hear that stops people beginning to invest is;

Investing is "risky".

In my experience, the people who don't have a "money tree" are risky, because if you have no investments (even small ones), you are usually a pay-check away from being bankrupt.

Investing is not rocket science, and you don't have to become a guru; you just need to educate yourself about the basics to begin with.

There is so much information available on the internet for free that we have no excuse in this day and age to be financially illiterate.

You wouldn't let your children grow up being illiterate, would you? Why would you let yourself and your children continue to be illiterate about your finances?

You can read so many fantastic books about any area of investing that takes your fancy. Heck, if you are seriously broke, then go and borrow some from the library or a friend.

Once you've done some research on a topic that interests you, find someone who is successful at it, ask them to lunch (you pay for it!) and ask them some questions about how they started and what they would do differently.

I am sure most of them would say I wish I started earlier and did not allow stinking thinking to hold me back.

The other thing that might surprise you is that successful people are usually glad to mentor someone who is keen to learn.

How do I know this? I have been on both ends of that situation. I have had many wonderful people mentor me in my investment life and have had the privilege of helping some people who I would now consider friends make their first venture into investing. You just have to be humble and ask.

10% of your income is for investing. This is paying yourself first!

INVESTING IS

Definition of investing from Dictionary.com Unabridged (v 1.1)

in•vest•ment –noun

1. The investing of money or capital in order to gain profitable returns, as interest, income, or appreciation in value.

2. A particular instance or mode of investing.

3. A thing invested in, as a business, a quantity of shares of stock, etc.

Just so we are clear with what an investment is.

Investing is putting your money into something that gives you a return.

It is building up an asset that grows in value and could be sold in an emergency.

I personally don't think your principle place of residence comes into this category. Because you don't actually generate income from it, and you may not want to sell it in an emergency.

My Dad would argue this point until the cows come home. Have you heard the saying, "Your own home is the best investment you can ever have"? The fact is if you or your parents were around in the great depression this would be a reality.

My Dad is a Baby Boomer, and he has done very well for himself by buying his own home. He has also not been an active investor, so this is true for him.

For those of us in the generations after them, this is not neces- sarily true.

I will however put one caveat on this statement: if you are a spender and you could not be bothered to become an active investor, buying a home of your own can be a great forced savings plan, and you will at least have somewhere to live when you retire.

EDUCATE YOURSELF AND SEEK ADVICE

So, if my house is not technically an investment, what is?

If you are a beginner, you might start with something like a Mutual fund.

Each year you get paid interest and a dividend, money made while you are sleeping, so to speak.

If you keep re-investing the dividend and adding contributions, the compounding effect helps to build up a nest egg to invest in other things that give you a bigger return.

Below is a list of a few of the thousands of different types of investments that are available today.

Real-estate	Stock market
Residential	Mutual funds
Commercial	Stocks/shares
Industrial	Options
Development	Futures
Foreign real-estate	Foreign Exchange

There is much more information available on my website, michellethemoneycoach.com

Find something that interests you and begin investigating. Do some courses, read some books. The worst thing that can happen is you find out you weren't that interested in that subject after all.

I spent one year studying a diploma course on options trading, I completed all of my assignments, passed all of my exams and did some paper trading. I decided that after all that, I did not love studying the stock market enough to be an options trader. However, I did learn a lot, I understand how to insure my stock portfolio, and I learned a lot about risk management and portfolio structure. Was all that study a waste of time? No way. I can use the knowledge in other areas of investing, and I can't say I didn't look at the opportunity with an open mind.

I am now studying foreign investing in real estate in the multi-family unit sector. I love real estate, and at this stage I am confident that this will be one of my next investing ventures. Having already gained experience in several other areas of estate investing, it seems like the next step for me.

I did end up investing in USA commercial real estate through a property fund set up by my Mentor, Steve McKnight. After all of my research I realized it was not easy to manage US property from Australia, so when Steve set up his fund I dived right in, because I knew the type of returns that were available and understood the value of his expertise and the combined buying power of many people. This fund is returning nicely and growing my money tree.

Many people are scared of investing because they have heard all of the horror stories other people tell. From personal experience, the times I have made bad investment decisions were when I was too lazy to do the research to educate myself about the investment and relied on somebody else's "advice", usually given at the dinner table over a few drinks!

Most of us are afraid because we don't understand.

"Knowledge is power." Get some!

THE OPPORTUNITY OF A LIFETIME COMES BY EVERY DAY; THAT IS, IF THAT IS YOUR EXPECTATION.

The challenge is that most of us are not prepared, either financially, mentally or skill wise. So, what most of us do is borrow to take the investment opportunity and because we are not "skilled" at investing, we can end up in a whole heap of trouble!

This is a risky person!

Investments are not risky, people are! There is risk in everything you do, life is risky, and no one is going to get out of it alive!

Risk is managed. Wear a seat belt, don't write your pin number down in your wallet, and look before you cross the road.

Learn how to manage risk.

I believe the most important foundation is a balanced budget.

Then, before you actually jump into anything, get some professional advice.

Personally, I have found that it is necessary to educate myself first.

- So that I know who to get advice from.

- So that I know what questions to ask.

- I know if the advisor actually knows what they are talking about.

- Sometimes it is just to make sure I haven't missed anything.

We have had well respected, heavily promoted "Advisors" tell us information that was incorrect, and had we followed the advice, we would have spent a whole lot of money for nothing.

It may take a few advisors to find one that is up to speed on what you want to learn about.

People (like me, for instance) can baulk at paying a few hundred dollars for advice because if they don't go through with the investment, it is wasted money.

In my experience, I have found that it is better to blow $300 on a consultation than to spend time and a whole lot more money on a business or investment and find a problem later.

Never rely totally on your advisor, either.

We have a friend who was telling me about their fantastic accountant who "handles" all of their investments for them. I voiced my concern to her at the time and found out just the other day that the accountant had misappropriated the funds from their investments and their friends' as well.

Be aware, and always understand what you are seeking advice about.

Due diligence is the key.

The other thing that causes many financial issues is the desire for quick riches.

I know I've been there myself. I have been looking for the quick and easy way to make money, all of my life, and I am now finally convinced that there is no such thing.

I see so many people running out to the back of the room at an investment seminar and paying thousands of dollars for courses on investing on their credit cards.

Buying negatively geared properties because the salesperson sounded good, and after all, you get a tax return.

Or borrowing money on credit cards to trade the options market. I have seen so much of this, and it horrifies me.

Don't get me wrong; I think it is really important to get educated before you begin investing.

However, the biggest mistake that I see is when people do not have their foundations solid, if you have not set yourself up with cash flow to invest, and you don't have a balanced budget with provisions, as we discussed in this book.

Then for you, any investment is very risky.

I believe it's not necessarily the investment that is risky, but the person who is risky.

Now that we have established what investing is, let's look at what it's not!

INVESTING IS NOT

Investing is not saving money up to buy a new car or to go on a holiday.

Even though the salesperson will tell you "your investment for this new car is only X dollars". That is just sales talk to make you feel justified in buying the car.

Take 10% of your income and invest it.

Once you begin the process, you will see that you don't even miss the money. After a little while you adjust, just like you do when you get a pay raise and you just don't know where that extra money went.

The thing you will notice is that the balance of your "wealth account" is going up, and you will soon be able to buy yourself an asset that makes more money while you sleep.

How do I know this?

Because I have lived it!

20 years ago, I was earning about $25k; I was single and living in a unit, had my credit card maxed out (I called it my sweat it card, because it was always $1000 above its limit), and I had car loan. I said to the person who was trying to educate me, "Look at my budget; I can't afford to take 10% of my income out, there's just not enough."

Thankfully, this very wise person didn't listen to my loser attitude and said, "With a budget like that, you can't afford not to!"

He said, "Why don't you just do it for six months and see if you can live with it?"

I am now saying to you, "Just do it!"

If you don't plan for this portion to come out of your pay check, it will just be frittered away.

10% SAVING / PROVISIONING
STOREHOUSE PRINCIPLE

It is important to understand the need to provision for unexpected things that might happen in the future, and the things that will happen, but you didn't plan for in your budget.

BE PREPARED FOR THE UNEXPECTED

Some of the things that will be provided for in this "bucket" are not so "unexpected".

Most of us just don't factor those occurrences into our budget/ money plan, because they don't happen that often, and we are usually budgeting for the here and now.

We are actually living one of those events right now.

Let me explain. Being the budgeting queen, I have provisioned in my budget for medical expenses and even for unexpected medical expenses of $500 per year. We are all healthy and have private health insurance. So, that should be plenty, right?

As I have a chronic injury, I have quite a lot of treatment which is provided for in our "medical bucket", so that is no problem. Where the plan came unhinged is, in February of this year, our 3 children all went to see a specialist of some kind; one to a Paediatric Dentist, the other an ear nose and throat specialist, and the third to a gastroenterologist, all costing between $250 and $400 per consultation. Long story short, the medical expenses for February were $1900. Thankfully, we have a great system in our country (Australia) called Medicare, and I was able to claim back $660 and some from my private health insurance, leaving $1235 of unbudgeted-for medical expenses for the month of February only. Oh oh!

Now that is not the end of the story. From the consultations and tests paid for in February come the expenses for the treatments to follow in March. My son has "hyperplasic" teeth; they look perfectly fine and have never given him any trouble, however, to stop problems arising in the future he required a general anaesthetic to have 4 crowns and 7 small fillings done, equalling $3500 in unbudgeted-for medical expenses. My daughter had braces fitted in April, requiring a $1600 down payment and a monthly payment of $200 for the next 21 months! Now that's about $6300 in 3 months!

If this was you, where would get that money from?

A credit card maybe! That would be the beginning of a very long merry go 'round ride!

This is one of the uses of your provisioning account.

Other things that could come into the "unexpected expenses" bucket are:

1. A medical emergency for yourself or a child.

2. A workplace injury- usually it takes some time for the claim money to come through and it is always less than you earn.

   Workers' Compensation, in most cases, it is about 70% of your income. Another thing that you don't find out until after the event is, if you are acting in a higher-level position than your actual job or you rely on overtime to build your income up, the insurance company will only pay 70% of your actual wage before overtime, and the position you are acting in does not count.

   How do I know this? I have been there.

   Read the small print on your policy!

   If you are having trouble now on 100%, what would life be like on 70%?

3. Car accident – even if you have comprehensive insurance, you will still need to pay the excess on your claim.

4. An emergency visit to a sick friend or relative interstate or internationally.

5. The funeral of a friend or relative interstate or overseas.

6. The loss of a job. I know it won't be enough to last forever, however, it could be the difference between keeping food on the table while you look for a new job.

   This is something we have also experienced.

When Glen finished work for the last time before he was out of work for 14 months, we had been practicing these principles for about 6 months and had paid off the last of our consumer debt about 1 week prior.

We thought he would find work quickly, so we prepared ourselves for 3 months without income.

We purchased a freezer and bought a 3-month supply of meat, and a 3-month supply of non-perishables, which we stored in our garage. Each week I would "shop" for the week's supply and bring it into the house. We also paid our mortgage, utilities and anything else we knew would need to be paid over the next 3 months in advance. We also paid the children's private school fees for the whole year.

We had a budget of $50 per week to spend on perishables like fresh vegetables and milk.

We had prepared for 3 months without income; however, we did not think it would actually take that long to be back to work. Imagine our surprise when he was out of work for 14 months!

If we had not:

1. Had a money tree as discussed in the previous chapter, and

2. Had six months of savings/provisions in the bank, and

3. Finished paying off our debt…

We would have probably gone bankrupt or, worse still, damaged our relationship with the stress, like many people we knew in the IT industry at that time.

Another unexpected expense that needs to be provisioned for is to;

REPLACE THINGS THAT BREAK DOWN

Now that's something most of us don't prepare for.

We forget that the towels we got as wedding presents wear out and need replacing. The sheets get holes in them, and the feather duvet begins to drop feathers all over the place!

The fridge and washer are only made to last about 3-5 years. Now I know sometimes they last longer; my dryer just died, and it was about 20 years old, but they don't make them like that anymore!

While Glen was out of work, we had many things break down, but because things were so tight at the time we didn't replace them until we had plenty in that account to cover us.

When my dryer died a few months ago, I just went down and bought one; no stress or worry, no credit that could not be paid back at the end of the month and, best of all, no robbing Peter to pay Paul. You know the old, I'll just use the electricity money this month and pay it back next month, meanwhile, one of the kids breaks a leg and we have a hospital bill to pay. This is how it used to be before, even though we earned a good income!

So many other things can go in this category. Just look around your house!

THINGS YOU UNDERESTIMATED IN YOUR BUDGET

Having this buffer allows you to have unexpected expenses and not blow your budget or get stressed out.

Most of the time when we do a budget, there are some things we forget to put into it, especially if they are things that don't happen often.

I guess you would say this is where you "could" do a little robbing Peter to pay Paul. Although if you are dipping into this account on a regular basis, you may have made some serious omissions from your spending plan.

If you have allocated every expense the way you have learned here, after the initial teething period of about 90 to 120 days is over, you shouldn't have to dip into this account very often at all.

EMERGENCY FUNDS

You never know what is going to happen in your life.

When our income fell from $160K down to $26k, we were shell-shocked.

If you had said to me a few months before, "What would you do if Glen were unemployed?"

I would have said, "There's no way he would ever be out of work. I have several contracting agents calling me every week asking me if Glen would be willing to break his contract, they would pay him whatever he wants."

Something you have to know about Glen is that he is a man of character, so he would never break his contract. That's just not him.

Thank God, we had been practicing the principles I am talking about in this book, including the debt reduction plan for about 6 months, before we had the opportunity to test out this concept.

OPPORTUNITY MONEY

Opportunity money is what you use when you see that deal of a lifetime.

Let's say you have something on your goal list. You may have begun to provision for it in your budget and you see it on sale for one-third of the price that it normally is. If you buy it now instead of in six months' time, you will be worse off.

You could use some of this money for that purpose.

I would, however, be very careful with this scenario if you are a spender, because if you are anything like me, I can justify just about anything.

Make sure your deal of the century does not deplete the whole account, or you will defeat the purpose of the account.

In the next chapter, I am going to discuss a dirty four letter word: <u>DEBT</u>.

DEBT: THE GOOD, THE BAD AND THE UGLY

Dictionary.com Unabridged (v 1.1)

debt –noun

1. Something that is owed or that one is bound to pay to or perform for another: a debt of $50;

2. a liability or obligation to pay or render something: My debt to her for advice is not to be discharged easily;

3. the condition of being under such an obligation: His gambling losses put him deeply in debt.

—Synonyms 1. obligation, duty, due.

Dictionary.com Unabridged (v 1.1) Based on the Random House Unabridged Dictionary, © Random House, Inc. 2006.

Now I know there is really no such thing as bad debt, as debt is a neutral concept, however the use of the term bad debt is more about whether the credit is used wisely or unwisely.

Used wisely, debt is the cheapest form of leverage when investing, and can multiply your profits immensely.

However, what you need to remember is that leverage is a double-edged sword. Compound interest, if it's working for you, is great, but when its going against you, it magnifies your losses. It is important to be educated so that you can manage your risk wisely.

If you are paying your credit card balance off at the end of the month and have no "consumer debt" (things like store cards with high interest charges) that is carrying a balance, then you are probably a person who can be "trusted" to use your credit card to make your day-to-day purchases and not carry what is called "bad debt". The reason it is bad debt is that it is spent on something that is consumed, or of little or no value that could be sold in an emergency if need be.

Personally, I am a spender and have gotten myself into lots of trouble with credit cards on several occasions.

Because of my past behaviour, there was a time when I first began using this system where I could not "trust myself" not to overspend, so I used only a debit card for my purchases for about 3 years to make sure I had totally broken the habits and would not overspend.

With that said, if you can be very honest with yourself and you can "trust yourself" to use a credit card, then the next section is probably not for you. However, as opposites attract, you may have a partner who falls in this category and you may still need to read on and figure out how to help them over the "habit".

If you are in the habit of not paying off the balance on your credit card at the end of the billing period, or you have any cards that are carrying a balance...

STOP USING CREDIT!

Yuck! That is the last thing you want to hear. And let me tell you right now from personal experience, if you are in the habit of using credit to pay for your lifestyle, this process will be quite painful for the first 3 weeks to 2 months.

However, it cannot compare to how fantastic you will feel when you have your finances under control and are moving into the positives of having excess cash flow.

It is so liberating to know when a bill comes in, like car registration, and the car needs fixing as well, you can pay for it and your lifestyle for the next month will not suffer for it.

My goal is to help you be free of debt slavery.

"But I'm not a slave," I hear you say. Oh yes, you are! If you have debt, you are a slave. How about that? You thought all this time you were a free person, but all along, you were a slave to debts.

Definition of slavery is: www.answers.com/topic/slave (reference)

1. One bound in servitude as the property of a person or household.

2. One who is abjectly subservient to a specified person or influence:

   "I can't afford to pay for health insurance because I have to pay the mortgage first."

   A mortgage gives the bank the right to recover their debt from you if you default. The fear of losing makes people act like slaves.

   It is an attitude.

3. One who works extremely hard.

   One who works or toils tirelessly: verb- To do tedious, laborious, and sometimes menial work:

   Who dares not speak his free thoughts is a slave.

   — Euripides (c.485-406 B.C.).

How about what the Bible says about it:

   "The rich rules over the poor, And the borrower is servant to the lender,"

   (Proverbs 22.7 NIV).

I have heard people say, "I can't let my boss know I am looking for another job in case he sacks me."

And, "I have to work overtime. That's what they expect of me, otherwise I am out of a job."

"I hate my job, but I have to stay there because I have a mortgage and credit cards to pay."

Can you relate to any of the above activities? I know I can.

Do you know anyone who works hard doing a job they hate, doesn't pay them what they are worth and fears losing that job, because they have debts to pay and might lose the house, the car and everything else?

Glen and I have made a decision in our lives that if we are in a situation where we might think this way, we are in too deep and need to change our lifestyle. When a man or woman has to put their job or another person above their family, then that is a debt with an interest rate far too high for us to pay.

We have a negatively geared property that is not performing, because the cost of the property has gone up by 50% and Glen's income has gone down by 25%. By choice, because he works less hours so that he can take the children to sport and go to the gym for his own health. The value of this property has gone down by $100,000, so we have decided to sell at a loss.

Why?

We could afford to keep it if Glen worked more hours and if I went and got a job to earn some extra income. However, he would not be able to go to the gym or sports with the children; if I was to go into the work force, I would have to give up my dream of writing this book and not be here when the children get home from school or go on their school excursions with them.

Being in debt takes away our choices.

Now don't get me wrong, when we were discussing this situation we did look at the option of me going to work and Glen doing extra hours; we actually wrote a list of about 10 ways that we could bring the extra money in, which we are also working on, instead of cutting our losses on the investment property. We put every option on the table. We even looked at selling our own home. This was a very emotional thing for me to contemplate.

You see, as a child I lived in 11 different houses by the time I was 10. The house that I lived in at that time was the longest house I had lived in until the house we live in now. Also, having lived in rented group share houses until I was married at the age of 30 has left its scar on me when it comes to having a place of my own.

The decision to sell the investment property came down to investment principles we have learned over the past few years that we have only just had the guts to put into practice. If an investment is not performing, you need to cut your losses early. We cannot see it improving, so if we put more money into it all we are doing is prolonging the pain and increasing the loss. With the benefit of 20/20 hindsight, we should have gotten rid of it 2 years ago.

Don't get me wrong, the decision to take an $100,000 loss was not easy; however, now that the decision is made, I am feeling relieved. We can always buy another property, one that makes good investment sense!

The property we are ditching would actually be a great deal for the person who buys it at the price we are selling it for, so I guess we will pick up something else in time to catch up in the next boom.

Long story short, we are in control of our financial situation, not someone else.

One way to make sure you don't slip back into old habits with credit cards is to **just CUT THE CARD UP!**

If that is too drastic for you, then there are plenty of ideas to help you not succumb to the temptation of using the card to buy a "great deal" that you see at the store.

Put it in water and freeze it, is one I've heard before. To add some extra protection you could freeze it in a tin, the reason being you cannot put a tin in the microwave.

You could store it in a safe or safety deposit box that you have to ask someone else, trustworthy and not a pushover, to get it out for you.

If you have any great ideas that we could share with

people, please go to my Facebook page facebook.com/ MichelleMoneyCoach and share your tip.

When I was using my frequent flyer credit card, I would just put everything on my card to get the points; the problem was I was overspending by $50-$200 per month, and @ 17.5% interest, I was constantly playing catch up. Not to mention paying fees and interest on a regular basis. My frequent flyer points ended up being very expensive!

Now things are very different; I actually earn interest on the money I spend. Last year I earned $500, and this year I'm sure will be much higher, as I now have compound interest working for me. When I originally wrote this book in 2008, Australian bank interest rates on savings were around 7.5%, which meant my earnings were pretty good. Now in 2016, the interest rates for most Australian banks are less than 1.2%. ING direct and Rural bank, the banks I personally use, are offering rates of 1.9% - 2.75%. Nowhere near the highs of 2008, however I still do ok from this because my bank balances are much bigger now.

You can do it, too!

My passion is to see as many people as I can take back the control of their finances and win the game of money.

DEBT REDUCTION

If you have debts, you might take some, about 5% would be acceptable, of your provisioning 10% and put that extra towards your debt reduction system.

If you are drowning in debt, you may need to also take some, about 5% would be acceptable, of your Investing 10% and put that extra towards your debt reduction system.

If you are seriously drowning in debt and you are having trouble keeping up with the payments, then you might need to get some professional help as well as implementing the steps outlined in this book.

A financial counselor may be able to help you figure out what you can do to "stop the bleeding", and negotiate a way out that doesn't damage your credit.

What most people do is put their heads in the sand and hope for the problem to go away.

Most creditors want to help you figure out a solution that benefits both parties. Because it costs them more money and costs you your credit-rating if they have to recover the money through bankruptcy.

I have found myself that if you can muster up the courage to phone them and tell them your situation, they will work with you, and if you tell the truth and stick to the plan it will not damage your credit rating.

When I was injured at work in 1992, I was in a very difficult situation; as a single woman with no family around, I had to support myself and pay my medical bills, while waiting for my case to be heard.

When I finally won my case, eighteen months later, I had racked up two thousand dollars on my "sweat it card" and a few small debts.

I was still unable to work and had to go on sickness benefit until I was well enough to go back to work. This benefit was only enough to barely exist on, so I would not be able to pay the credit card or anything else off, so I had to come up with something that was win-win.

I worked out whom I owed money to and determined what percentage of my total debt their debt was, and then I rang them and told them the whole story.

I told them that as I was going to have just enough to survive on, I would not be able to pay my loan payments once this happened.

"My loan with your company is X percent of my total debt. I have just received a payout of X dollars, so I would like to propose that I pay you X dollars if you would waive the rest of the debt and not affect your credit score."

To my surprise, some companies will accept less than half of what is owed to them.

If you do not ask, you will never know.

If you wait until the collection process begins, you have less bargaining power. Always, always, keep the lines of communications open with your creditors. If you lack the confidence to do it yourself, then seek the help of a financial counselor.

TWO OF THE BIGGEST MISTAKES PEOPLE MAKE WITH DEBT

The number one biggest mistake I see people make is sticking their head in the sand and not negotiating with their creditors, as I discussed in the previous chapter. As with any relationship, communication is the key.

The second biggest mistake I see people make is to focus on the debt and want to get rid of it quickly, without looking at the big picture, of developing a money management system that takes your whole financial situation and your future plans into consideration.

They reason with themselves. "If we take the 10% savings and the 10% investing money and pay off our debt, we will get out of debt quicker and then be able to save up to invest."

Oh, sure you will!

The other issue with this way of thinking is you might have no debt or less debt. However, you will have nothing to fall back on in an emergency. Then what do you do, rack up more debt?

Let me save you the heartache; it will not work. Otherwise, you would have done it already.

If you are thinking, "I did do that; I have paid my debt off," and are back in the hole again and vowing to pay it off again, you are dreaming. You know I am telling you the truth. I have been there too.

Think about this: what are you focusing on?

You are focusing on the debt.

If you are focusing on the debt, it is a sure-fire subconscious affirmation to keep you in debt.

What you need to do is set up an automatic debt reduction plan to pay it off.

In addition, you could find a way to make more money, not necessarily by working longer hours though, as that might cause you relationship issues if you are taking too much away from the family.

There are many home-based businesses that can be operated on a part-time basis. You can benefit from the tax advantages of having a business as well as earning a pretty good income part-time alongside your 9-5 job. The other advantages are you don't need a lot of capital, skill or experience to begin, and the good ones have teaching and motivation systems to help you grow yourself and your business. I have friends who are doing very well in this type of business; in fact, they have done so well they no longer need their full-time jobs.

Open up your mind and think about the things you want in life, dream a little, if you never try you will never know.

A paradigm shift is necessary, and it will pay off big time.

This is important, because many people will short-change themselves by looking at paying off the debt quicker.

If you do not change your habits, you will still end up exactly where you were before, except with even more debt.

It's a bit like dieting after each one you put a little more weight on and it is harder to get off!

In the next chapter, I'll show you how to set up an automatic debt arrester.

THE AUTOPILOT DEBT REDUCTION SYSTEM - "DEBT ARRESTER"

If you have debt to get rid of, we have developed a tool to help you. The Debt Arrester system is the most effective and painless way to get out of debt and stay out.

1. Face the music – dig out all of your loan statements. Look at:

   The balance;

   The interest rate;

   How much interest you are paying each month.

This can be a very sobering experience.

I have had some clients who have been paying 20% interest on $20,000 of credit card debt; they had no idea how much it was actually costing them.

This, believe it or not, is very common. It was advantageous for them, and may also be for you to:

 - ➢ Call the credit card company and ask for a lower interest rate.

 - ➢ Check out credit card deals that offer a balance transfer at a lower interest rate for the life of the balance.

Note: It is vital that you read the small print on this type of transfer. Often all is not as it seems. Sometimes a higher interest rate for a longer period or higher annual fee can skew the outcomes, to such a point that because of the fees, the higher interest is a better deal than the lower.

Be careful: you must **never miss a payment.**

Never ever buy anything on this card or you will be in even more trouble than before.

You must also **destroy the card** that the balance was transferred from so that you won't be tempted to use it. Otherwise, you will be back on the merry go 'round again.

2. Work out how much of your income is going to go towards debt reduction, over and above your minimum payments.

   A good rule of thumb is 5% to 10% of your net/after tax income, or half of your 10% provision and investing amounts, as discussed in the previous chapter.

3. Enter all of your debts into the Debt Arrester form.

INSTRUCTIONS FOR DEBT ARRESTER FORM

Line 1: Debt name: to whom do you owe the money?

Line 2: Balance remaining: The current balance owed. If you are unsure, give your provider a call and ask for a payoff figure.

Line 3: Minimum monthly payment.

Line 4: Interest Rate.

Line 5: Payoff priority.

The priority is determined by starting with the highest interest rate from line four. This determines which order to pay the debts off in.

The highest priority is the debt with the highest interest rate.

Note: There are two schools of thought about the order in which to pay off the debt in this type of system. One is pay the debt with the highest interest rate and lowest balance, and the other is the one with the highest interest and largest balance. The main difference in the two systems is the psychological benefit of paying the smaller debts off quickly to give you a feeling of success.

4. Once you have determined the payoff priority set up automatic payments to pay the minimum payment on all of the debts except the number one debt. To this one you will add the extra money allocated to debt reduction to the minimum payment.

   Make sure you have an idea of how many payments it will take to pay number one off, just in case you forget and over pay.

   The way this works is all of the debt is paid on autopilot, so you are not focused on the debt. The minimum payments keep the payments under control and you have the "creative head space" to think about making more money, rather than reducing debt.

   Psychologically, it makes sense to be thinking about something positive. And, when you do have a windfall, you can put that into the mix as well.

5. Once debt number one is paid off, take the minimum payment and the debt reduction funds that you were paying on debt number one and apply it to debt number two's minimum payment, and then when that is paid off, do the same thing with number three. On and on until you have cleared them all.

The most exciting this about this system is the momentum that develops as you move through the cycle.

Now you can begin to look at ways of earning some extra income. There is plenty of opportunity out there if you open your mind.

Once you have the right "mindset", you will realize that money is not difficult to make.

We are constantly uploading new information to our web site, so please go to michellethemoneycoach.com to get some up-to-date tips on reducing your debt.

70% OF YOUR INCOME IS FOR LIVING ON

Pay all of your bills and expenses out of this amount, including loans, mortgage and car expenses.

Below are some of the categories and expenses we have come across in helping people set up their spending plans, to help jog your memory about things you might spend money on but might forget about when coming up with a spending plan.

LIVING EXPENSES

Childcare

After school care

Bus and train fares

Dry cleaning

Gas & parking

Entertainment (Adult pocket money)

Mad money

Lunches and coffees

Cleaning products

Groceries

Fresh fruit and veg

Meat

Gym membership

Newspapers & magazines

Personal needs (hair care, waxing)

Sport and Hobbies

School lunch orders

School excursions and camps

School sports

Language classes

Swimming lessons

CD's & games

Singing/dancing lessons

Pocket Money (kids)

Books

Cigarettes

Alcohol

Tip: Most of the things in this category will be paid for with cash, so I use my debit card for these expenses.

UTILITY EXPENSES

Rent

Electricity

Gas

Rates - general/land/water

Telephone

Prepaid Mobile

Tip: We make the payments for utilities on autopilot by setting up periodical B-pays, remitted to the utility company weekly or bi weekly as our wages are paid.

GENERAL

Holidays

Gifts

School fees

Education

Clothing

Savings/ provisioning 10%

Conferences

Work and union fees

CAR

Insurance

Maintenance

Registration

Unexpected expenses/ a new car (10,000) in 3 years' time

INSURANCES

Ambulance

Medical & Dental Expenses

Income protection

Private health insurance

House & contents

Life/trauma cover

Superannuation

UNEXPECTED EXPENSES

House repairs & maintenance

Medical & dental

Other

Tip: We make the payments for everything else on autopilot by setting up periodical B-pays remitted to the supplier or deposited into a high interest zero fee bank account specifically allocated for it. This autopilot payment happens on a weekly or bi weekly basis as we receive our wages and builds up until the money is required for the bill.

This is how I make money on the money I spend. Last year, I earned $500 in interest using this system.

LOANS

Minimum loan payments

Student loans

Mortgages

Car loan

Credit card

Loan

Tip: This group is paid according to the previous section on debt reduction, using automatic B-pays and direct deposits.

Remember the loan repayments come out of the 70% for living expenses, plus the added extra funds allocated as we discussed in the previous chapter.

We do not actually have any of these bills ourselves.

INSURANCES

It is vitally important if you have any debt at all, and especially if you have a mortgage, to have all of the necessary insurance policies in place, even if you are a single person. It is even more important if you have a partner and children.

We have had many clients who have sat down with us to set up their budget who say, "I can't afford to pay for life insurance or income protection." In fact, I even had a friend who started a small business and she said she could not afford to insure her business.

I know it is expensive and I know the chances of having a claim are slim in most cases, however I also know you can't afford not to have it. Because if you can't afford the protect it, you definitely won't be able to come up with the money to replace it should anything go pear-shaped.

When one of our clients, who had a huge amount of debt and a husband self-employed in a dangerous industry, told us they could not afford insurance, I said, "You can't afford not to have it. You need to put those expenses into your budget first, along with the big rocks."

If the unthinkable did happen, how would your family survive?

How traumatic would it be if your children had their home foreclosed on, as well as having lost their loved one?

HOME & CONTENTS OR RENTER'S INSURANCE

A few years ago, there were terrible fires in and around Canberra, the city where I grew up.

Some friends of mine lost their houses, and others had the fires stop at their back fence. A very scary time indeed.

Five hundred houses burned down.

Surprisingly, many people had not insured their homes or their contents. So not only did they lose all of their possessions, they had to find hundreds of thousands of dollars to build a new house, as well as tens of thousands to replace their possessions.

Some of these people were in their retirement years. With limited income, having owned their homes for many years, they thought they did not need to have them insured. Yes, they were thankful to escape with their lives; however, they were traumatized by having to start again at a late stage in life, for the sake of a $300 insurance policy.

LIFE/TRAUMA COVER

We have Glen insured for enough to cover all of our debt, with enough left over for the children and I to live comfortably for several years, without the need for me to go out and find full time work.

When our income fell by 84%, it was very difficult for us to keep paying the premiums. We had a trauma policy that, if allowed to lapse, the replacement product would be significantly less effective. Therefore, we did everything we could to keep it going.

PRIVATE HEALTH INSURANCE

Having told you earlier about the thousands of dollars in unbudgeted medical expenses for us this year, you know I am going to tell you how important private health insurance is. Especially hospital coverage; if we were not covered for the operations two of our children had, our out of pocket expenses would have been beyond our reach. Even though we have a great system in place to cope with emergency funds, we would not have been able to make it work.

We would have had to say to our children, "You will just have to put up with it until we can afford to pay the ten thousand dollars for your operation."

INCOME PROTECTION

Income protection is critically important for anyone who is self-employed, because there are often expenses associated with a business that, if you were incapacitated and the business stopped producing income, would still need to be paid.

I personally think everyone needs this type of insurance.

Many people say to me, I don't need income protection because I have worker's compensation through my job.

If you have an injury at work, you "may" be covered by your worker's compensation. However, if you have an accident outside of work or have a car accident not covered by worker's compensation (i.e. not going to or from work), where is the income you used to earn going to come from when it can take several years for cases to get to court?

If the average person is only a pay packet away from bankruptcy, how is your family going to survive and also afford to pay for your extra medical treatment until you "win your case", if you do win it?

Because a large percentage of bankruptcies site accident or injury as the cause of the financial difficulty, it pays to make sure you are covered adequately.

AMBULANCE COVERAGE

Most private health insurances cover Ambulance. It can also be purchased separately for a reasonable price if you don't have private health insurance.

If you are injured, it can cost a hefty price to be taken a short distance in an ambulance.

I have always made sure I had this insurance, because I have heard many horror stories about the cost of an ambulance trip.

Only a few months ago, I had the unfortunate opportunity to use my coverage. While at the local shopping centre, my 13-year-old daughter choked on a small candy. It was policy of the shopping centre management to call an ambulance. The paramedics treated her and asked if she wanted to go to the hospital. My daughter did not want to go to hospital, as she was fine.

About one month later, I received a bill for $285, and she didn't even get in the ambulance. Imagine how much the 12 km drive to the hospital would have cost! My insurance covered the full cost.

I am not a financial planner and I don't know your individual circumstances, so if you are unsure what insurances you need, talk to your financial planner.

While I am talking about life and death matters (pardon the pun!), while it is not really part of budgeting, having an up-to-date will is a very important part of your financial planning. If you don't have a will, get one done now!

STEP TWO
PUTTING THE 'BIG ROCKS' IN PLACE

"PUT THE BIG ROCKS IN THE BOWL FIRST!"

Have you ever seen the big rocks demonstration?

If not, go to michellethemoneycoach.com/big-rocks-video **and watch the video.**

Below is a pictorial representation of the Big Rocks Principle

Do you think all of the things on the table will fit in the round bowl?

As you can see, if you don't put the "big rocks in first", they definitely will not fit.

When you put the "big rocks" in first, it all fits beautifully.

The fish bowl full of rocks

Big rocks first:

The big rocks represent the important things, like giving, investing and saving.

Pebbles:

They also represent important things, such as life insurance, health insurance, income protection, food, shelter and clothing.

Sand:

The sand represents all of the little things we spend our money on. Some of them are not essential.

This might be where you can do some tweaking in your budget.

To me, the water represents the fact that there is always more you can do, even when you think you cannot do any more.

There is always space to fit some water into your budget!

Personally, I have found that this is where you experience **the God factor**.

When our income fell from $160,000 down to $26,000, at first, I could not get my head around how I was going to make ends meet with such an enormous change in our financial situation.

What I found was, if I did my part, God would do his part according to his word.

"For I have learned to be content whatever the circumstances. I know what it is to be in need, and I know what it is to have plenty. I have learned the secret of being content in any situation," (Philippians 4:11, 12 NIV).

"My God shall supply all of your needs according to his glorious riches," (Philippians 4:19 NIV).

We experienced many amazing miracles during this time, and still do.

PUTTING THE BIG ROCKS IN:
THE BIG ROCKS ARE YOUR FOUNDATION

ACTION STEPS FOR THE BIG ROCKS

1. Set up a high interest, zero fee account for each of the big rocks, and name them accordingly.

2. Set up a periodical direct deposit of 10% of your net income to go automatically into each of the accounts.

Don't kid yourself and say, "I'll start it after I pay the electricity bill." From experience, I know that you will not do it later, because there will always be something coming up.

Do it now!

If you are waiting for the ducks to line up perfectly before you begin, you never will take the shot.

Action steps for the Pebbles

1. If you don't have the correct insurances, do some research and/or go and see your financial planner.

2. While you are at it, check that your wills are up to date; if not, update them immediately.

3. For the insurances that have annual payments, set up a high interest, zero fee account for your insurances.

4. Set up automatic internet banking direct deposits or B-pays for the insurances that are paid monthly.

If you have any questions about the process, please visit me on Facebook at facebook.com/MichelleMoneyCoach or michellethemoneycoach.com and ask a question.

STEP THREE
ACCOUNT FOR YOUR SPENDING

ACCOUNT FOR WHAT YOU ACTUALLY SPEND IN EVERY AREA

Let's face it; we all would love to live on a champagne budget, but when reality is beer or water, this is disastrous. I know many people, in fact I was one in the past, who are going backwards financially by as much as $200 per week.

We can kid ourselves that it is ok, but eventually it catches up and you have to clean up the mess. It's better to go through a little pain of adjustment than to kid yourself and have to clear a huge debt, or even go bankrupt.

This is not theory. It is what we do and have done to get through our own tough times and found that this works even on a very low income!

Pull out the bills, a notebook, and spreadsheet; whatever works for you.

Work out what your real expenses are.

You will need to **account for everything**.

Often when we do a budget, we account for most things and fudge the rest.

This is ok if you have plenty of money left at the end of the month, but not when you have month left at the end of the money!

If you are a spender like me, if it is in my spending account, it will be spent!

What if you don't know what your real expenses are?

Let's face it; most of us don't know what our real expenses are, so you are not alone.

Below are a few things you can do to find out.

> You could get a note pad, keep your receipts, and write down every cent you spend for two weeks to one month.

  This is a very sobering thing to do; it sure made me realize how much money I waste and what useless junk I blow my money on.

> Another thing that you could do, if you mostly use a card to pay for things, is just keep your receipts for a few weeks, making sure you get a receipt for absolutely everything you buy and add the receipts up at the end of each day.

  It is important to add up the receipts at the end of each day, because by the end of the week you might forget what the receipt was for.

> You could do a grand total for the week, multiplied by 52, and add 20%, if you were pretty sure the week was a typical week's spending.

  By keeping the receipts, you have an idea of what the things that you spend discretionary money on are, and you can put them into your spending plan.

  What I did when I had to get real was swap to using a debit card, which is also called a secured credit card. This type of card uses your own savings, but acts like a credit card.

  Now for some people this will be difficult, as we have all been trained to use our credit cards, to avoid fees and to get frequent flyer points.

  When you are using credit cards all the time, you are usually at least one month in arrears. Therefore, when you start to use the debit card, the first few months will be a challenge, because you have to catch up on your past.

> **Most importantly, stop using the credit card.**

Sometimes you can find deals where you can do a balance transfer at a low rate for the life of the balance. There is often a catch to doing this, and you need to read the fine print very carefully. The other mistake people make is to do a balance transfer and keep on spending. That is not how you fix this situation.

If you cannot be trusted with credit, then just cut the card up.

If there has been a little "financial infidelity" in your relationship, this might be a little bit of a challenge for you, because you have been hiding your discretionary spending from your partner.

Well, you are about to get naked with them! Once you have both seen the naked truth of your spending habits, you can forgive each other and both work together on a spending plan that fits the needs of both of you. Once you get rid of the financial infidelity, you will have less guilt and less stress.

It is very important that you account for everything, or your automatic money machine will not work as well as it should.

LOOK FOR LEAKS

Leaks are the little things we spend money on that do not seem to be very big until you add them up over time. They are usually things you buy impulsively and forget to account for in your spending planning.

This is an area where you may be able to find a few extra dollars to put somewhere else in your budget if you are in a tight spot.

Think about things like that cup of coffee you buy on the way to work at $4.50 a cup, 5 days a week. That adds up to $22.50 per week; that's $1170 per year.

What if you were having two or three coffees a day? That would be $2300-$3500 per year. I have friends who would easily have that many coffees a week.

That equates to $45-$67.50 per week. If $50 per week invested over 7 years at a measly 7% returns $23,000, do you think you could change a few habits and think about your more prosperous future?

What about cigarettes? In 2016, a pack of cigarettes in Australia is around $25, OMG!! if you smoke a pack a day, that's $175 per week and adds up to $9100 per year. Now that's almost what I paid for my new car last week. If you are a smoker, you could totally change your financial future by quitting. I believe there are also lots of helpful services available to assist you. Before you get all narky with me, I should tell you I was once a smoker. I quit 25 years ago, so I know it is difficult to do; however, the rewards are more than just financial, as the health benefits are enormous. If you are in the USA or another country, the prices may be a little lower, but relatively speaking the effect is still the same financially and with your health.

If you think you can't afford to put money away to invest, then maybe you need to rethink a few things.

Now I know you don't want to give up all of your little luxuries, however if you have credit card debt and/or no money to put towards your money tree, maybe you could consider changing the habit a little. For example, maybe you could buy the regular size and only have it 2 or 3 times per week. Alternatively, you could buy a cappuccino maker and make it yourself at home before you leave.

It is fine to have some little luxuries; we just need to make sure they are in the spending plan. A few little leaks can add up to a large river of dollars at the end of the month, especially if there are two of you.

How about the take out on the way home from work, and take out lunches?

The average lunch in the city where I live is at least $12.50 for a sandwich (nothing fancy) and a drink. Do that five times a week, times two people, and there is $125 bucks a week.

My husband has lunches that his work mates envy. They often say, "So what are you having today? It smells great," as he heats them in the microwave.

He goes shopping once a month and makes up great meals with frozen vegetables, chicken and beef with several different sauces. They cost him about $40 a month and take him less than an hour a month to make. He puts them in the freezer and takes one to work each day. He sometimes even pays our daughter to make them for him.

By the way, girls, did you notice that he goes shopping and makes them himself? He always loves his meals because he chose them and made them himself!

Another little side note, our children have made their own lunches since kindergarten and I have never had a complaint about what is on the sandwich or a moldy sandwich found in the cupboard or school bag.

It just goes to show that we all like to be responsible for our own little piece of the family chores, so if your husband or kids are whining about your cooking, you know what to tell them!

Back to the spending leaks. How about DVD rentals and DVD overdue fees?

I got stung the other day after renting some DVD's for my son's birthday party. I took them back 1 day late and it cost me $9 in late fees, and that was half price because I paid them on the spot. I almost had a nosebleed! The kids didn't even watch the darn DVD's!

Have a think about the things that you may just pick up along the way each week, like;

Bottled water, soda pop, gum, magazines, lottery tickets, extra pocket money for the kids, lunch orders, pizza delivery, and gifts.

Speaking of school lunch orders, I know people whose kids spend $3 a day for lunch at school consisting of hot chips and sauce; not very nutritious, but they like it. Think about this: $3 a day for three children over twelve years is $48,000. When invested at 7%, now there is a nice chunk of the college fund that you thought you could not afford to have.

I'm sure if you pitched it to the kids the right way, they would prefer to be healthy and not having to work as hard while they go to college, and not to have a huge school loan at the end of it.

I hope you now have some ideas about where to look for some savings to make your future brighter.

Once you have accounted for your spending and plugged your leaks, it's time to collate the information into a spending plan.

NEGOTIATE A SPENDING PLAN

Once you know what your real expenses are, and you have broken them down into categories, it's time to put them all on the table, or should I say Bill Bannisher, and negotiate the plan.

Make sure you include both wants and needs, because life gets boring when you can only have what you need and have nothing to look forward to that you want.

It is important, though, to understand the difference between the wants and needs. If times are tough, you can still put the wants in the plan, but instead of getting them this year, you might have to wait a little bit longer for them. At least you know you are working towards something positive.

Have everything on the table, and then negotiate what is important to all parties.

In our travels, we have seen all kinds of unsatisfactory situations:

There is the situation where one partner is handling all of the money while the other partner has to beg for every cent they get, while the money-managing partner is not accountable for anything they spend. That is no way to have a happy and harmonious relationship.

Or the situation where one partner is spending money on credit cards that were not agreed to, and the other partner has to clean up the mess when spending gets out of hand.

All of the indiscretions need to be put on the table and

negotiated. This is important. There needs to be a plan and money rules that are acceptable to all parties.

The way to handle an out of control spender is not, "Right, you are going on a budget and this is the way we are going to do it, and that's it," unless you want some espionage happening in your relationship.

It is important to have some rules; they must be acceptable to all parties, and they must be fair.

I believe the reason why we have never fought about money is that we had some rules right from the beginning.

I have never worked outside the home since we have been married. I have had my own businesses that I have worked from home; however, the majority of my income comes through Glen. We have always shared the financial responsibilities.

I have my own account in my name, as well as my own credit card and a joint credit card. There are certain parts of the budget that I look after – clothing, medical expenses, my car, half of the savings, half of the holiday money, food, and groceries. Glen looks after all of the major household expenses.

We both have a certain amount of money, which we can spend guilt-free. In addition, we are not accountable for that money. If I blow it on junk, that's my problem.

I rarely have to ask him for money and if I did, it would not be a problem because he is a kind and generous man.

The only time I think he would have a problem is if I was being irresponsible and running out of money constantly because of my behaviour.

If that was to happen, and it has in the past, we would have a guilt-free discussion about why I think I am having a problem managing. Then we would work out a plan together.

Now, it would be a different story if I were running out constantly because there was not enough coming in to cover my expenses. The process would be the same, but the plan to resolve it would be different and would involve a revision of the whole financial situation of the family.

Another rule is that if either of us is going to spend more than $100 on our joint credit card, we check with each other. The attitude is not, "Can I have permission to spend $150," it is, "I'm going to spend $150 on this; is this OK?"

I also have a rule of my own. That is, I never buy anything on my credit card that is not provisioned for in my "provision buckets", never! If I have $300 in my clothing account, I know I can spend up to $300 on clothing on my card; if I only have $50 in that account, then I know that if one of the children needs new shoes and they cost more than $50, they will have to wear holey shoes for another week.

COMMUNICATION IS THE KEY.

When you negotiate, it needs to be done in a no-blame manner, even if someone has stuffed up and landed you both in trouble. Forgive each other and move on; you are both part of the same team.

DO IT TOGETHER.

If you have other problems with communication in your relationship, it might help to have some sort of professional help from a counsellor as you go through this process.

I will be talking about Bill Banisher in the next chapter. We have found that it is a great tool for couples with communication issues to use in putting the big picture on the table, so to speak.

I helped a couple recently where the husband was the income earner, making a reasonable income. The wife was a stay at home Mom and had all of the financial responsibilities without access to the income. He was not giving her enough to cover the expenses she was responsible for, and he was spending money on whatever he felt like as well as racking up debt on a credit card, which she had told him she was very unhappy about. Communication in this relationship was very difficult, as the husband did not seem to listen to her, even though she tried to tell him how she felt.

The Bill Banisher tool enabled them to sit down together and see in living color what was going on in their lives financially.

The other benefit it had was that it was not her telling him that he was doing things wrong, it was the program and the "trainer" showing him the reality of their circumstances. No blame!

He then made a choice to change.

About a month later, I got an excited call on the phone from the wife saying how thrilled she was about her future. She could see how they might one day be able to buy a home of their own as they had money in the savings account, something they had not been able to do ever before in the fourteen years they had been married.

Negotiate who is going to manage which bills and provisioning accounts. As I discussed earlier in this chapter, both partners should have some responsibility for managing the finances.

In the next chapter, we will cover creating your spending plan using my Bill Bannisher system.

STEP FOUR
BILL BANISHER

DEVELOP YOUR SPENDING PLAN

Now we are finally at the point where the rubber meets the road.

- ✓ You know the money rules.

- ✓ You know what your expenses are and have factored in the things you were not providing for in your budget until now.

Now you are ready to do that dirty six-letter word: a budget.

Before you get all shaky and lightheaded, we have developed a budgeting tool to help you with this process.

Because you have purchased this book, you have access to the basic Bill Banisher budgeting tool free of charge.

This is my special gift to you for taking the time to read my book and implement the system.

What you need to do is:

Go to michellethemoneycoach.com/basic-bill-banisher and fill in your name and email.

Read the Bill Banisher user guide instructions.

1. **Fill in the net income you receive from all income sources. We are talking about your after-tax income for this spending plan.**

   If you do not know what your net cash flow/after tax income is, grab a calculator and work it out. Take your gross before tax income and subtract your tax and superannuation.

2. **Put the big rocks into your spending plan first.**

   Giving 10% of income

   Investing 10% of income

   Saving / Provisioning 10% of income

In case you are thinking, "Are you insane, how can I live on 70% of the 100% I already can't live on?" and you are feeling a little bit of stress right now, let me put your mind at ease: **The 10-10-10-70 is optimum. That is our goal.**

It is a good idea to start with the optimum 10% amounts to begin with.

If your budget does not balance and you have debt, you can then tweak the figures in the giving, saving and investing, but only after cutting expenses.

I believe in cutting expenses before cutting out the big rocks. The big rocks are very important to your long-term goals for financial freedom, and if you shortcut this step you will short-change your outcomes.

Just like if you add a drop of kerosene to your cake mix, the cake will not taste quite right.

If you have credit card debt right now, you are probably not going to be able to achieve the exact model we are using straight away.

Isn't it great to have a goal to reach for!

If you cannot do ten percent, then do five percent; however, it is important to make sure you have "something" going towards each area; giving, investing and saving.

I know you are thinking, "I just can't do that," or, "I'll wait until after the electric bill comes," or any of a hundred excuses. Don't fool yourself and listen to the voice of doubt and procrastination.

You can do it, and you need to do it now!

Even when we were on government benefits, while Glen was unemployed, we were practicing these principles, but it was more like 5-5-7-83 percent. I don't tell you that to stroke my ego; what I want you to get your mind around is that changing a few habits will definitely change your financial future. Do what you can today to set your foundations up, and aim for the optimum in the long term.

Here are a couple of possible variations:

So, you think you can't do 70/30 because you are drowning in debt.

Try tweaking it a bit:

- 5% towards giving
- 10% towards investing
- 5% towards saving/provisioning
- 10% towards debt reduction
- 70% living

Or

- 10% towards giving
- 5% towards investing
- 5% towards saving/provisioning
- 10% towards debt reduction
- 70% living

Just give it a try. You will find the right mix for you and your life, and the most important thing to remember is you must plan for the expected and the unexpected, and you must be working towards having a money tree of your own. It will never happen if you don't start it now.

3. Enter your expenses into the expenses tables.

This is where you will use the information gathered in the "account for your spending" phase in step 3.

4. **Work out your payment schedules.** The schedule will give you a hard copy of where the cash will be flowing and gives you the details required to set your automatic payments.

> Check your schedules to make sure the cash is flowing to the correct accounts.

You can find more information about the schedules at michellethemoneycoach.com/schedules

WHAT IF MY BUDGET DOESN'T BALANCE?

Once you have worked out all of your outgoing expenses, you may find that the numbers in the cash flow table of the bill banisher are **red** or negative numbers.

There are a couple of reasons for this.

1. **You are spending more than you earn** and are going backwards without realizing. This may be a wakeup call for you. There may be a little "pain" to bring into order.

I know, I have been here too! Remember, no pain- no gain.

Maybe you have a champagne taste on a beer budget.

You will need to rearrange a few things in your expenditure to bring it into line.

When you are tweaking your expenses, please don't forget

the principles we have been discussing all through this book.

Please try to keep the big rocks as close to ten percent as you can. Cut your expenses first. If you keep your foundations strong, you will do much better over the long run.

If you neglect the universal money rules, you will still be in the same rut in one year or ten years' time; it will just be a lot deeper.

The good habits keep your foundations solid.

2. **You have substantial debt to clear** to make your expenses fit the new budget.

You may need to "tweak" the 10%'s for a short while, but only after you have adjusted your spending first.

If debt is your problem, go back and reread the section on debt reduction. In addition, if you need help, get it.

Follow the debt reduction plan to the letter.

Don't be tempted to say to yourself, "If I just put all of the 10%'s on my debts, it will clear them faster."

Remember you are developing new habits, and if you have not gotten rid of your debt before, chances are you will not be able to stick to it now.

This is not theory. When Glen was unemployed, he joined a government program called NEISS. Because of the way it was structured, I lost the government benefit I was receiving.

I had already cut our expenses to the bone and was now facing a $120 per week drop in income. I still stuck to my principles of giving, investing and saving, but they were reduced a little, something like 7%,5%,5%.

During that time, we never had a bill that we wondered how we would get the money to pay.

We also had money in the bank for emergencies, savings and investment money of about six hundred dollars once it was all over. Six hundred dollars is not much, but it is a start!

Once you get your foundations in order, you will never be behind again, as long as you don't slip back into old habits.

If there are **no red or negative numbers** in the cash flow table of Bill Banisher...

CONGRATULATIONS!

You have balanced the budget and are now wondering what has been happening to the money that you are now giving, saving and investing.

Well done!

You are going to be streets ahead in no time!

5. **Next step is to set up your autopilot banking accounts.**

SET AND FORGET

This is where we take the information gathered and the negotiated plan and put it to work. This process has probably taken you a couple of hours. If you have calculated your spending plan well, you should not have to change anything unless something changes in your financial situation.

That's it; you are done. Your finances will be on autopilot from here on.

NOTE:

Make sure that you have read the fine print on all of your accounts. You must understand any fees that could be charged, including transaction fees and any fees that might occur if there are insufficient funds. Don't just assume anything! We have found some accounts that do not charge any fees for insufficient funds, and others that charge exorbitant fees.

It is helpful to draw how the cash flows through your spending plan. It works a little like a machine when the cash flows around it. You need to know how the money flows before you set your auto payments.

To do this, you will need to:

Make a list of all of the areas that your budget is broken down into.

If you used Bill Banisher, the schedules will give you the details. This list makes up the accounts you will be setting up.

Decide what account your income will go into.

Do you already have an account that you want to use, or do you need to open a different type of account to avoid fees or have more flexibility for automated bill payment or internet banking?

Now is the time to bite the bullet and find the right accounts for your needs. You may need to open one or more new accounts; you may even need to change banks.

Far too many people are not happy with their current situation but think it's too hard to change. Now that you are ready for change, set up what you need now. Once you have the system running, it is on autopilot, so you should not have to think about it again for a long time.

Once you realize how easy it really is to change, you will wonder why you didn't do it sooner.

Perhaps your income will go into what we call a clearing account.

A clearing/dispersing account is an account you use to distribute the cash flow to the "provision buckets" that represent each area of your spending plan.

The one I use has high interest, zero fees, allows periodical online payments to anyone and allows periodical B-Pays to the utility companies. It does not have a card or a check facility; it is an on-line only account.

I have only been able to find one account like this at this stage.

Do some investigating; it is amazing what you will find out if you ask questions. Some banking institutions don't promote these accounts; you have to ask for them.

There is plenty of information on the internet. You can go to my website MichelleTheMoneyCoach.com and checkout my Facebook page facebook.com/MichelleMoneyCoach.

If you have found a good account that we have not mentioned, let us know. I don't know everything, but I'm sure between us we can find the answers we are looking for.

ARE YOU GOING TO USE A CREDIT CARD TO PAY SOME OF YOUR EXPENSES?

Tip - Remember if you are in debt or an out of control spender, it might be an idea to think twice about using a credit card until you have your automatic spending plan working successfully without using credit.

Decide who is going to manage which bills and provisioning accounts as I discussed in the previous chapter. Each partner needs to have some responsibility for the finances of the household. This is for many reasons, but the important ones are so that they can feel in control and know how the family finances work.

Too many people, especially women, are left in the dark until either a tragedy like the death of their partner or a divorce forces them to figure it out.

CHOOSE THE ACCOUNTS YOU WILL BE USING FOR YOUR "PROVISION BUCKETS".

You may need to do some research for this. There are several websites with plenty of information available.

Go to MichelleTheMoneyCoach.com and find updated information and tips on this subject.

Put the Big Rocks In

10% Giving

"Giving or blessing others is great for your self-esteem and for your finances."

Set up a direct deposit or some kind of automatic internet banking payment to your worthwhile cause where you are in charge of determining how much and how often you give.

I use two methods of giving here; I have a giving account that is a high interest, zero fee account where I keep a balance for giving, as well as having automatic direct deposits set up with my gifts going directly into the bank account of my worthwhile causes.

10% Investing

"Investing is putting it into something that gives you a return."

Plant Your First Money Tree

Are you excited? This is the beginning of your new future.

Set up your high interest, no fee bank account and call it your 'investing' or 'money tree' account.

Set up your automatic internet banking payment so that 10% of your income goes into this account.

Begin educating yourself about investing. Think about what type of investing interests you the most. Subscribe to free newsletters. Visit websites. Ask questions.

Don't just talk to people who are selling financial products or services. As my website grows, there will be lots of information about investing; go to michellethemoneycoach.com and have a look.

Your first investment should not involve a substantial amount of debt, and you must have a written plan.

10% saving / provisioning

"10% of your income is for saving / provisioning."

Remember this "provision bucket" is for replacement of depreciating items, furniture, things that break down, a rainy day, goals and dreams.

Having this buffer allows you to have unexpected expenses and not blow your budget or get stressed out.

Set up a high interest, zero fee account and call it Saving / Provisioning. Set up your automatic internet banking payment of 10% of your income to go into this account.

If one of your goals requires funding, (such as an overseas trip), then set up a separate savings account as well as an automatic payment for your big goal.

70% Living

"Pay all of your bills and expenses out of this amount, including loans and mortgage and car expenses."

How many "provision buckets" you will need to have will depend on the level that you want to break your expenses down to.

As a guide, set up 7-9 high interest, zero fee bank accounts.

Set up automatic internet banking payments to direct the money from your clearing account into your "provision buckets" according to the areas of provision you created in your Bill Bannisher spending plan.

SET UP AUTOMATIC PAYMENTS FOR UTILITIES.

For the utilities and other regular bills, use the schedules created by Bill Banisher to set up automatic payments and remit them to the utility companies as you receive your income. It's a bit like paying as you go. This way you never have to think about paying your utility bills again. The best thing is that the utility companies keep track of your payments for you.

The utility company lists the payments made on your account statement. In the months when usage is lower, our account gets heavily in credit, so that when the usage increases in, say, winter, a $532.32 bill is covered with $173.53 remaining to build up for the next high usage period. How would you feel if you received a bill in your mailbox for $532.00 now?

The majority of our bills come in with please do not pay in big letters along the bottom.

It is a great feeling to never have to worry about paying bills again.

Where having your utility accounts in credit might be a challenge is if you are renting and/or move around a lot. In this case, it might be better to have a zero fee, high interest account for utilities and automatically send the money there each payday, then pay the utilities according to the account. **You must never dip into this account to help you cover other expenses.** No robbing Peter to pay Paul from this account, no matter what.

BANISH YOUR BILLS

Once you have set up your automatic online bill payments, you can say good-bye forever to lining up in banks, post offices and stores, writing checks and even sitting at your computer to pay your bills.

Alleluia!

I have been using this system for nearly seventeen years now, and as technology improves, it just keeps getting better every year

By now, you have realized that this system is perfect for people with no self-discipline and a lazy streak, like me.

In the past five years, I have only been into a bank about 3 times, and that was to deposit some cash and a check I had received, and to exchange some money to travel overseas.

I am amazed when I walk past the people lined up outside the post office for half an hour. I think to myself, do these people not know that they don't have to do that? And as I continue to work with people, I realize it is true most people don't realize they do not have to do it, that there is a better way.

My passion is to spread the word and help thousands of people each year discover how to free themselves from the burden of debt, the pain of fighting about the lack of finances and the hassle of managing their household bills.

Let's forget about our finances, and focus on the fun!

STEP FIVE
IMPLEMENT BANKING SOLUTIONS

MARRY YOUR BUDGET TO YOUR BANK ACCOUNT

Marrying your budget to your bank account makes it **unnecessary to have self-discipline or skill.**

The biggest reason for failing budgets is the fact that the cash flow is not married to the budget.

If the budget is not married to the cash flow, then the budget is destined to fail.

Why? Because you never really know how much you can freely spend.

Most of us, and I include myself in this basket, lack the self-discipline to set up a budget and stick to it.

This becomes even more of a problem if there are two of you using the same account. This leaves us open to overspending, because we don't all walk around with a budget in our head, and sometimes the other person does not necessarily know what bills are coming up and what is coming out of the account. This challenge is also compounded if we are married to someone who has a spending personality opposite to ours. This can be frustrating and cause arguments, which is why we have created this program; to avoid arguments, and to make managing your finances effortless.

In our relationship, I am the spender, which if we didn't have this system running would mean that over the years, we probably would have had fights over money. I am pleased to say that because we have been managing our money this way all along, we have never actually had an argument about finances!

Once you have opened the necessary accounts and set up the automatic payments discussed in the previous chapters, you have officially married your budget to your bank account!

Now the bank will take care of your budget!

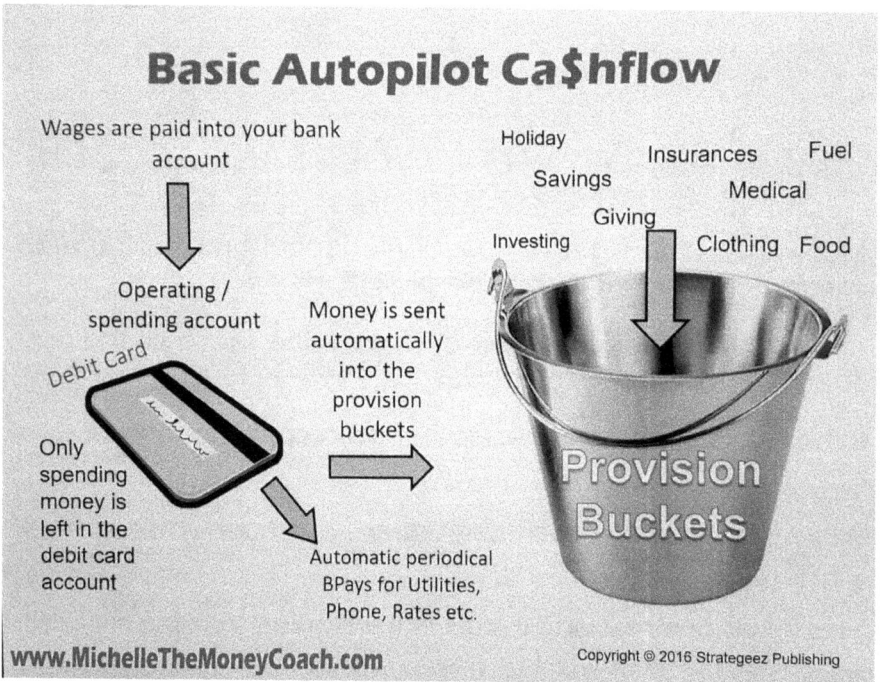

Basic Autopilot Ca$hflow

Wages are paid into your bank account

Operating / spending account

Debit Card

Only spending money is left in the debit card account

Money is sent automatically into the provision buckets

Automatic periodical BPays for Utilities, Phone, Rates etc.

Holiday
Savings
Investing
Giving
Insurances
Medical
Clothing
Fuel
Food

Provision Buckets

www.MichelleTheMoneyCoach.com   Copyright © 2016 Strategeez Publishing

USE TECHNOLOGY EFFICIENTLY AND COST EFFECTIVELY.

Fee free, high interest online bank accounts

The banking system has changed considerably in the last 15 years or so, which makes it a great time for us to be able to set our finances up efficiently and cost effectively.

There are, however, a few tricks that you need to learn to make sure that you get exactly the right accounts set up for your needs.

We are looking for high interest bearing, zero fee accounts. These allow us to divide our money up into provision buckets, so that we can easily see what's available in every area of our spending plan.

Why? So that we know, without having to look at our budget, without having a spreadsheet, without having to walk around with a head full of numbers, exactly how much is available to buy that new handbag, that new power tool, clothing for the kids or even just service the car and pay the registration. Without guilt or stress, or your partner saying...

Is that drill new? Hmmmm...

Is that a new handbag? Hmmmm...

What about the electricity bill!

In the past, the bank fees and transaction costs made it very difficult to use the banking system to manage your budget. There are now no excuses!

In 1999, a very progressive international bank began marketing their online savings accounts here in Australia, and around the world prior to 1999.

When we first developed this system, they had the only zero fee, high interest bearing accounts available, and that's what we used.

I have nine online savings accounts; they are the "provision buckets" for each area of my budget.

Over the years, other banks started to market accounts that looked like the online savings. However, there were often catches, like, you needed to have a $4000 balance in your main account to get the higher interest and not make any withdrawals from the account within a month.

There are some things you need to know before you begin setting up new accounts to budget the autopilot way. Make sure to **read the small print about how the accounts work**.

Everything is not as it seems! The questions that need to be asked are:

Is it truly fee-free?

How do you get the money out?

Do you need to have a minimum balance in another account?

Is the high interest paid on every cent in the account?

Is there a penalty for withdrawal from the account? For example, some accounts don't pay the higher interest if you make any withdrawals during the month, and you must deposit a certain amount each month.

Does the money need to be in the account for a certain amount of time?

A term deposit (that would be a CD in the United States) is not the type of account we are looking for.

Can I pay anyone or B-pay from the account?

The financial system is a bit of a minefield in the area of these accounts, and as we are not financial advisors, just educators; all we can tell you is what we have done ourselves.

There are many other accounts that we have used, and we are constantly testing out new accounts that we find, and that other people who use our system tell us about. Please visit MichelleTheMoneyCoach.com for up to date information, or visit us on Facebook facebook.com/MichelleMoneyCoach.

Transaction/ Debit Card and Checking Accounts

There are a couple of things you also need to know about the account you are using as either a clearing/dispersing account, or your operating/spending account.

1. You need to know if either of these accounts charge fees to do electronic (internet) transactions. If they do, either change to one who doesn't or change the way your cash flows.

2. Do they have internet banking facilities?

   Can you set up automatic payments using their online banking facility? Does the online facility allow automatic bill paying services?

3. Some banks use clever marketing to entice you into accepting low interest rates on your money to avoid paying account-keeping fees.

   For instance, if you keep $4000 in your account at all times, they will pay a slightly higher rate and you don't get charged any fees on the account.

   Don't be fooled; before you accept this type of deal work out how much you could be earning if you paid the fees and had the money in a high interest, zero fee account. You may be very surprised.

   Don't just accept it; do some research and find one that gives you what you need. And don't be afraid to change bank accounts.

4. You need to know what other fees and charges your account has.

   Is there an exorbitant fee for overdrawing your account? Not that you are going to set things up that way, however, sometimes things don't go quite as planned.

Always read the product disclosure statement carefully.

I hope by now you have completed the steps to financial freedom on your current income and are on your way to a prosperous, debt and stress free life. Remember, once you are ahead, you will never be behind again as long as you continue to develop good money habits.

CONGRATULATIONS!

From now on, all you will need to do is check that the system is ticking along nicely.

Make sure you are not paying too little or too much on any of your automatic payments.

That's it; no more budgeting the old-fashioned way.

You should never have to worry about those expected or unexpected expenses again.

I wrote this book so that you can be free from the stress and hassle of making ends meet, and to help you to prosper no matter what your income.

I pray you are now on the path to realizing that vision.

Now that you have your foundations in order you can begin start thinking about adding an income accelerator to your income sources. An income accelerator increases your ability to produce extra income that doesn't require you to exchange hours for dollars and provides extra funds for investing to produce more passive income, giving you even more freedom to choose your own path in life.

Visit my website and book in for the latest webinar series that will help guide you to prosperity.

We love to hear of your success stories, so please share yours with us, and if you have any questions, make sure you go to the web site or facebook and get them answered.

MichelleTheMoneyCoach.com

or

facebook.com/MichelleMoneyCoach

To your prosperity!

Michelle

www.ingramcontent.com/pod-product-compliance
Lightning Source LLC
Chambersburg PA
CBHW070736220326
41598CB00024BA/3444